Strawberries and Cream

by
Mary Rose Hayfield

Mary Rose Hayfield

Published in Great Britain by
Beloved Warwickshire Products

Mary Rose Hayfield,
Maengwyn House,
Maengwyn Street,
Machynlleth,
Powys,
SY20 8EF

ISBN 0 9513501 5 3

Computer set in 11 on 12.5pt
Palatino by
Phil Williams
Tegfan, National Street,
Tywyn, Gwynedd, LL36 9DB

Printed by
Artists Valley Press,
Birmingham House, Machynlleth,
Powys, SY20 8BG

Illustrated by Mary Rose Hayfield.

Beloved Warwickshire Products

First Edition 1996

ISBN 0 9513501 5 3

For John and Margaret Johnson
and all the happy
memories
of Church Farm, Shustoke, Warwickshire.
Long Ago.

Author's Preface

In my story, "Strawberries and Cream" the Radfords at Hill Farm have moved into the sixties. It is still a family farm, but times are gradually changing and family farms are beginning to seek extra outlets and more acres.

Peter the Radford's nephew joins the farm staff and a lovely redhead comes on the scene.

The midland countryside is as full of birdsong and flowers and woodland and green fields as ever. Winter and Spring, haytime and harvest come and go in their due season. The strawberries ripen and Mary Radford makes them into jam. Howard and Ling have a little daughter, but some things never change. Cows must be milked morning and evening, come what may. There are good days and bad days, but the Radfords have farmed here for close on two hundred years. Their feet are planted as firmly in Hill Farm soil as the oaks in the front fields.

John and Mary Radford are the roots of those oaks, and the very essence of the happiness within this family.

Do come with me again along the lane to Hill Farm, and in the fields, and along the footpath through the woods near the reservoir. Where the swans are nesting and the moorhens and and wild duck are dabbling among the reeds. And where at dusk the little bats fly free, and the owls hoot softly in the oaks near the farmhouse.

VIII

STRAWBERRIES AND CREAM

Chapter 1

Snowbound

STRAWBERRIES AND CREAM

Chapter 1

Snowbound

Mary Radford bent her ample back over the Aga oven, pulled open the door and lifted out the tray of mince pies. They smelled delicious and she gave a little sigh of satisfaction. Pushing back her hair from her hot forehead she turned and placed the pie tray on the big pine kitchen table along-side three other trays also full of cooling pies. Mary went to the sink and rinsed her hands before setting out the cups for her menfolk's mid-morning drink. She filled the kettle and put it in the hotplate, put the tea in the big old teapot and stood waiting until the kettle boiled. Then she made the tea and left the pot to keep warm on the top of the cooker. Turning back to the table she took up the old short-bladed kitchen knife and began to lift the cooling mince pies onto the wire tray which was waiting at the ready. Before she had finished she heard the menfolk coming across the yard. The back door opened and her son Howard came in knocking the snow off his boots beyond the mat as he came.

"Gosh that's a good smell Ma." Howard leaned his tall figure forward to pinch a mince pie.

"Don't you dare." Mary yelled, "Touch those and I'll thump you. There's tea and new buns for elevenses. Those pies are for Christmas Eve."

Mary heaved her bulky frame in it's warm blue work dress between the tempting pies and Howard. Behind her glasses Mary's eyes twinkled however and her love for Howard showed clearly in her broad smile. Her husband John followed Howard into the farm kitchen, and winked at Howard, as he hung his cap and coat behind the door. He flicked his fingers through his white hair.

"Your Ma's getting real mean with her pastry, never lets me get so much as a taste until it's served on the table. It's a wonder I'm not as thin as a rake by now." John laughed out of his blue eyes as he spoke.

"Get away with your nonsense you two. Teas brewed and the new buns are in the safe on the blue dish. Reach them out Howard dear, and the butter dish while you're about it." Mary lifted the tray of mince pies and carried them away into the big pantry. She was soon busy pouring tea while the men sat down and buttered a bun each. John rarely ate between meals, but the day, a few days before Christmas, was bitterly cold. An icy wind from the East had cut through both men's coats, giving even John an appetite for a tasty snack. They all sat for a few minutes enjoying the warmth of the kitchen. Both men looked real countrymen. The hard life of farmwork, day after day, year in year out, showed in their rough hands and weather beaten complexions. John Radford had farmed Hill Farm's 176 acres all his working life. Stockily built with blue eyes and fine hair which had turned prematurely grey in his late thirties, he was rarely seen without his pipe. He pulled it out of his pocket now and began to refill it from his pouch.

John's son Howard was in many ways like his father, but tall and slim. His eyes, green instead of blue, were shaped just like Johns. The dark hair, like his mother's was untouched by grey, it curled against his neck and about his ears. Married now for some years, he was still deep in love with his wife Ling, and his life centred around her and their two children, and the old cottage across the fields where they lived.

"What a dreadful morning. Never do I remember bitter weather and snow like this before Christmas. Usually it comes in January round here." Mary grumbled cheerfully about the weather as she poured the second cups.

"How'd you go on with the sheep then? Are they all off the hill?

"Yes we got em all down with the bribe of a bale of green hay." Howard answered her as he stirred his tea.

4

"The old dog would never have faced the drifts in the top field, it's as well we left her here, and that the ewes came to Howard's shout. It's still snowing heavy now." John heaved his bulk out of his chair and went to the window. Outside the wind whipped flurries of snow onto the deep drifts which lay against the stackyard wall. The yard was a white desert across to the cowsheds and the new cubicle houses and milk parlour beyond. Beyond that again he could see the long line of trees, branches clad white with snow, moving to and fro in the cold wind.

"After dinner we'll need to get the snowplough out and run the tractor up and down the lane and down to Ling in the cottage .... I can't see the Council clearing round these minor roads. Wonder how Charles and Gorse are faring? I bet the snow piles up across that field road of theirs. I expect the Council will clear their main road but the milk tanker will need to get across the fields to the house in the morning." John was talking about his son Charles' farm which was some miles distant.

"Damn good thing they went for a bulk tank last year .... easier for the milk tanker to cross the field than for Charles to dig out last nights churns from a snow drift. That's if it's as bad as here."

"I don't see how we can get over there anyhow. How about giving them a ring Lass to see how they're going on?" John turned to Mary as he pulled on his coat and cap to brave the weather once more.

"Surely, I'll phone after dinner. Now see you come in to dinner on twelve o'clock John. Don't get stopping out in this cold too long." Mary was anxious about John who was not so young these days.

"Never fear Ma, I'll see we knock off in good time, I'm for getting milking done a bit early and getting back to Ling and the kids in good time. It looks like being a hard night if this snow keeps on." Howard reassured his mother with these words and a bright smile. They opened and closed the door on gusts of wind and falling snow. Mary, left in the house, washed up the cups and put the saucepan of potatoes on to cook and a stew-jar full of beef stew in the oven to heat. Fetching an apple pie from the pantry she set it in the slow oven to warm. Next she mixed a jug of custard to make later. Then she laid the table for dinner and went through to the sitting room to kindle the fire to make a cosy welcome for the afternoon and evening time when John would come in tired and cold.

"Thank goodness we've plenty of kindling and coal in the little house shed near to hand. But what about Ling and the kiddies in all this snow?" She turned all these thoughts over in her mind as she worked. Presently the tasks were complete and the midday meal sending out good smells of meat and gravy from the Aga oven. By twelve noon Mary was at the door to open it and brush away the snow from the back porch. Snow was still falling and John and Howard had white flakes melting upon their coats as they came into the warm kitchen. They shook out their damp garments and hung them behind the door.

"Oh good to be in the warm Lass." John pulled off his wellies and pulled up his chair at the table after a quick hand wash at the sink. Howard was also glad to get in out of the weather. He had arranged to have dinner at the farm while the weather was so bad. Normally he walked home to dinner at the cottage through the fields and beech woods beyond, but it was hard going in deep snow.

"I'll give Ling a call after dinner, just to check that she's OK and see how much snow she's got." Howard cleared the last mouthful of stew and pushed his plate away, stretching his long legs under the table.

"Yes Dear do do that. It is such a lonely feeling, all the snow everywhere, and the woods so silent, no one about anywhere. I'd go for a walk over there in my wellies, but I think the hens will take me all my time until dark, with the snow still falling too." Mary looked quite anxious, Ling and her little boy and girl were very close to her heart.

"You stop here Love, no sense in you falling in the snow that won't help anyone. I'll see Howard gets away early and our Ling will rest quite content if Howard phones her after dinner.

Anyway on I may get down there with the snowplough just now."

John's plate was also empty and Mary got up to clear away the plates and serve the apple tart with plenty of hot custard. While the men ate she made fresh tea and poured three cups. Soon they rose to go back outside.

"What are you on with this afternoon? Are you round the yards?" Mary asked as they pulled on their coats.

"Yes I'm going to bed all the cattle down and grind some barley in the barn, then have a trip down the lane with the snowplough. Howard's going through the back to take bedding to the sheep and unfreeze the water troughs. Mainly it's all keeping the stock going until this weather clears off. It can't thaw too soon for me. I don't really hold with snow falling before Christmas." John smiled as he spoke.

"Nor I, if it doesn't finish soon we'll never get any holly picked for Church at Christmas or a tree for the house. Imagine climbing up the hill in this to get a fir cut in three feet of snow." Mary replied.

"We'll send young Howard." John grinned at his son as he spoke. "He'll soon wade up there, he could take the old sledge and come back down the hill Father Christmas fashion."

"OK Dad I'll do it if you'll milk Christmas morning."

"That's no trouble now we've got the parlour and the bulk tank Lad. Even with more cows, we soon get through em." John was smiling broadly now.

"When I remember how I had to argue you under the table to get you to agree to the new cubicle house, let alone the parlour, who's talking now?" Asked Howard as he moved through to the hall, where the telephone stood on a little table. A few moments later he was back.

"All's well at Bunny Warren. Sally Anne's asleep in her cot, and Richard's out making a snowman under the apple tree. Ling's cleared the path to the back gate but the lane's getting filled up with drifts. She hasn't heard any cars on the main road all day but I reckon the snow will have blocked off the sound.

Council will surely have cleared and gritted the main road?" Howard looked questioningly at his Father.

"God knows, they're as tight for money as anybody else these days. Anyway let's get the stock seen to and then we can get old Nuffield and the snowplough organised Lad, and I'll have a go at a trip down that way to see what's what." John moved to the door as he spoke.

"Fancy little Richard out in this, I hope he's warm wrapped, but of course Ling will see to that." Mary said as she looked out at the snow still falling in soft big flakes.

"He's mad on snow that one, and doesn't seem to feel the cold." Howard drew his scarf about his neck and zipped up his storm jacket against the cold, making for the door as he spoke.

As the two men went out Mary went to the phone. She spoke to Charles' wife Gorse and was reassured to hear that a Council snowplough driver, working on the main road, had agreed to run his machine up and down the drive across their fields to their buildings in exchange for hot drinks in the farmhouse kitchen. As soon as she had put down the phone Mary tidied up then muffled up in warm clothes and wellingtons went down the orchard to her poultry pens. She went armed with the fire shovel to clear the pen doorways. It was a cold white world but Mary was helped by the fact that Howard had made a way down the orchard to all the nine hen pens so she was able to get fresh straw, buckets of feed and clean water to each in turn after clearing the steps off with the shovel. She was soon busy about her work, keeping warm by keeping busy.

Down the lane John was battling with clearing drifts across the roadway. Looking up across the fields he could see the outline of the old mill and the pines and firs along the skyline. In the fields between, great snowdrifts curled in fantastic rolls and scrolls. The snow still fell but lightly now not obscuring his vision.

"Never get up there till this lot shifts." John muttered to himself as he rounded the bend and was in sight of the main road. He saw at once that it was clear and gritted. He breathed a sigh of relief and steered the tractor down the last fifty yards of lane. The return journey was easy now that he had a way cut through. In all he went up and down four times making the way clear for the bulk tank to come in next morning to collect the milk.

"That's if it stops snowing soon, looks to be getting less and the sky seems to be clearing." John squinted up into the snowflakes still falling. With the lane now clear he turned the tractor along the main road for a short distance turning right into the grassy lane, now snowbound which led to Howard's cottage. John turned the tractor and setting the snowplough as high as he could headed straight into the first big drift. The plough pushed it steadily away as though slicing through butter. Soon he reached the cottage gate and here his daughter-in-law and young Richard were waiting to welcome him with open arms. Richard, now nearly five years old, was tall, a small replica of Howard. At the moment he was jumping up and down with excitement.

"Grandad, Grandad, what a big spade you've got on the tractor. Can you clear the snow? Can I have a ride on the tractor? Have you seen my snowman? Where's Nanny is she coming?" Out tumbled the questions, hardly heard above the roar of the tractor engine. John raised his hand and continued fifty yards further down the lane to where there was room to turn and guide the machine back up to the gate. Here he stopped and climbed down.

"Well Lass if I go up and down a few times, that should let you all get about again a bit easier. So long as we don't get another fall tonight."

"Well come in for a cuppa, a hot drink will help keep out the cold." Ling opened the gate to welcome him. Richard caught his hand and dragged him across to see the snowman in an old black hay-makers hat to set off his coal button eyes.

"Can I have your pipe to put in his mouth Grandad?"

"No you can't young fella, you can have an old one out of Nanny's drawer when you come up to the farm later on."

In the cottage kitchen, Sally Anne, John's youngest grandchild sat in the pram, delighted to be made a fuss of by her Grandad. She was a chubby little morsel with dark curls and brown eyes and a serious expression. John stayed to drink a welcome cup of hot tea then left to finish clearing the lane.

"Thank you Dad .... so much .... it's lovely to feel joined on to civilisation again."

"Cheerio Lass, wait and see no more snow comes before you make too many plans for tomorrow." John was back on the tractor and setting off to do a few more bouts with the snowplough before setting off for home.

After a long tiring cold day Mary and John were in the sitting room either side of the fireplace with a good fire crackling between them and the old dog asleep at their feet. Howard had gone off with his milk-can at dusk, via the road as the easiest route. Young Bill, the lad who worked at the farm had helped John put the cows through the milk parlour and feed them hay in the cubicle houses before settling them down for the cold night ahead, with fresh litter under each cow they looked well-cared for and comfortable. The men had closed up all doors tight and stuffed sacking in the calfpen cracks to keep all the young stock as warm as possible in the bitter weather.

John stretched out his legs to the blaze appreciating the comfort after the discomfort of the hours outdoors. He picked up the farm diary off the side table and laid it on his knee. Taking up his pen he began to fill in the days events in his neat copper plate handwriting. Mary sat opposite him quietly knitting a little jersey for one of Charles' twin boys at River Farm. A few minutes later she looked up, specs twinkling in the firelight as John spoke.

"You know Love, the finance of it all doesn't get any easier .... I'm thankful we've moved to parlour milking and can now handle fifty percent more cows, but there are a lot of questions to be answered you know."

"Oh John Dear, I do wish you didn't always have these money worries .... we are lucky in a way you know .... our Ling and Gorse, and I as well of course, don't want a lot of expensive things. We are happy with the children and our men-folk, without too many luxuries. It's a way of life to us you know. And to our boys as well. A way of life we all love and wouldn't swop for all the tea in China." Mary smiled lovingly as she spoke.

"Oh Lass, I know that, but it's not that that is going to cause us trouble. It's the whole trend towards BIG is beautiful in agriculture that is sweeping across the country. The real question is, will we be able to keep our heads above water with 176 acres? Will Charles be able to raise a family on much less ground? It's my belief that we shall only maintain what they now call "A Viable Unit" if we branch out and find some new lines .... diversify they call it nowadays. One thing I'm damn sure of is that we shall have to box carefully. The sixties are not going to be as easy as the fifties. There's five little lads in the family now to work for. Young Richard, Bill, and Charles' little twins may all want to come on the farm for all we know. Even Jim's boys may be interested later on." Mary thought for a while before replying.

"But John, Jim and Kitty will have plenty to provide for providing for their two, and some or all of the other four may not want to come on the farms." She raised her eyes questioningly to her husband's face as she spoke.

"I know that Lass, but I'm the head of the family, and as I see it, whatever we decide over the next two or three years will decide our fortunes for years to come." John's face held little lines of worry as he spoke and brought instant response from Mary.

"Well Dear, I don't think you do have to carry all the load yourself. Howard and Charles and our Jim are all clever lads with good heads on their shoulders. Kitty's always been a well educated young woman. Ling's a live wire, a real good "farmer" in her own right. Gorse is a wise steady wife and mother. they are all so sensible and full of common sense, in their own different ways. D'you know what I think Love?" She ended smiling up at him.

"No Lass, you tell me. I'm always guided by you in the end." He reached across and laid his hand on her shoulder.

"I think you ought to tell them all your hopes and fears .... consult them. After Christmas is over we could start the year with family gathering to pool everyone's ideas. A family conference. Then the worries would be shared amongst us all. Much better I'm sure. I know nothing at all about viable units or diversifying but I do know our children and their lovely wives. they will all be full of good ideas .... I'm sure of it." Mary settled back in her chair and watched John's reactions to her point of view. A slow smile spread across his face, he picked up his pipe from the mantle shelf and lighting a newspaper spill from the jar, he bent his head to pull with his lips on the pipe stem. As he laid the spill across the bowl he grinned across at her. When he had the pipe well lit he leant back in his chair puffing contentedly.

"You're a wise Lass you are. I think you may be right, sometimes it's hard to realise they are grown men and women. We'll have ... what did you call it? A family conference. A new year pooling of ideas among the whole family. It might be quite something quite enjoyable all round Lass." John lay back and closed his eyes to enjoy a pleasant doze by the fireside before bedtime.

STRAWBERRIES AND CREAM

Chapter 2

Christmas Comes and Peter Comes

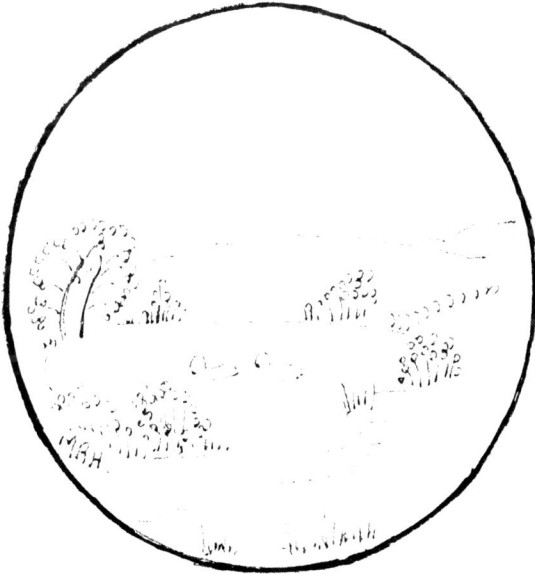

STRAWBERRIES AND CREAM

Chapter 2

Christmas Comes and Peter Comes

Early next morning Howard was due to milk at Hill Farm. He and his Father took alternate days so as to give themselves an extra hour in bed every other day. Howard was up early and after making Ling a pot of early tea and taking it upstairs he stayed only to drink a cup himself, then he slammed the cottage door behind him calling up the stairs as he went.

"Bye Love, see you later." As he crunched down the snowy path to the now cleared lane, and thence on to the main road he felt that the weather was on the change. In spite of the weather men on television having stressed the likelihood of cold weather continuing, it seemed to Howard that it was warmer today. When he reached the main road he was sure of it. The hawthorn hedges were dripping gently even though it was still almost dark. The lad, Bill was amongst the cows when he got to the farm.

"Hello there, I think it's a lot warmer at last, do you?" was Howard's greeting.

"Aye I do that .... quite soft by our back compared to last evening." Bill grinned cheerfully. He had grown into a tall fair-haired, blue-eyed young man, well built and strong-armed. He was a useful and reliable member of John's staff now and compared with the gangling, runny-nosed kid of a few years back, he was a credit to John's training. He was very good and quiet with the cows, and the two men quickly opened up the parlour and had the first eight cows in the standings with the milk clusters on and the pulsators pumping the milk along the pipeline into the bulk tank. Howard washed the cows bags and let down their feed into the automatic hoppers while Bill moved fresh cows in after each batch were milked and moved on. There were just on seventy Jerseys to milk but it took them just over an hour to finish. It was a far cry from the old cowshed system when each cows milk had to be carried up to the cooling house by hand.

The old cowsheds had been adapted for calf pens by John and Howard a year or two before. Each standing was now divided into two small concreted pens each with it's own door and small rack for hay in the corner. When John came across from the house milking was finished. He brought two steaming mugs of hot sweet cocoa.

"Warmer is it? Feels warmer to my old bones. Praise be." was John's opening remark.

"Yes, we both think so, and no more snow fallen. Anyway I'll get to the sheep, if you and Bill can finish here. Parlour's been washed and the units done."

"Yes OK son, you get to the ewes, we'll feed the calves and young stock, see you at breakfast." John heaved up a green hay bale, cut the strings with his penknife and began to put wedges of it into the calves racks. Bill began to mix powdered milk for the calves in the sterilised buckets in the old cooling house, now nicely kitted out as the calves feeding pantry. All three men began the daily tasks of Winter time livestock care on the farm.

Indoors, Mary and Wanda the old dog were in the kitchen. The dog lay quietly by the stove while Mary laid the table ready for breakfast and put a tray of bacon to simmer in the oven. She sliced bread and heated the frypan on the hotplate, putting in a good sized knob of lard. When it was hot she moved it over to the Aga slow-plate and brought a bowl of eggs from the pantry shelf. She broke half a dozen into the hot fat and left them to simmer gently. By the time the kettle was boiling, milk and butter and marmalade laid out, toast in the rack, tea in the pot, and John's orange halved sugared and segmented in his dish beside his place, the three men were coming in at the door.

"Morning young Bill, morning Howard." Mary smiled her welcome.

"Mam says can the young uns have a go down your hill with

their old sledges, afore the snow's gone?" Bill had a family of young brothers and sisters growing up fast behind him.

"Surely Lad as long as they shut the gate and don't skive off school to do it. Or has school finished for Christmas?" John glanced enquiringly at Mary as he asked the question.

"School ends today until after Christmas, Mrs. Hilkin was on the phone for a bit of holly but she knows we can't get it unless the snow goes." Mary replied. Mrs. Hilkin, the headmistress of the village school where Radfords had attended for generations back, was an old friend. John and Mary were both school managers. Usually Mrs. Hilkin was given a nice bunch of berried holly to decorate her home in Sutton Coldfield before Christmas.

"Well we may be able to get holly and trees yet Lass, it's certainly thawing this morning." John rose from the table and went to tap the weatherglass as he spoke.

"Goes down a shade, so maybe the snow's on the way out." He stood looking out of the window at the grey lowering sky.

"Could turn to rain before long." John sat down at the table and began to butter a slice of toast, he never ate a cooked breakfast. The lad, Bill and Howard were by now tucking into plates full of eggs and bacon and fried bread. Mary served herself a smaller amount and settled in her chair to enjoy her breakfast.

"I hope the packing station can get their new van through to pick up the eggs. I've got nearly three boxes full this week. The pullets are laying really well now in spite of the cold. Those big pens, plenty of food, and being such a good strain of bird .... that's the reason I'm sure."

"And your rearing and care Ma .... that's surely a lot to do with it." Howard spoke between mouthfuls.

"Well the Black Leghorn / Rhode cross has always done me well here. I know the eggs are white, but sending them to the packing station it's no odds whether they are white or brown. It's only if it's for farm gate sales that they need the extra attraction of being brown. Now Charles with his main road position must produce brown eggs, but he doesn't get as many eggs per hen as I do. We were discussing it only last week." Mary got up to refill their cups as she spoke. She loved keeping the poultry and making it pay. She felt it was a way of helping John with the farm. He never touched her egg money but most of it was spent on food and clothes and extras for the family home.

"Well I'm going to suggest that after Christmas we all meet, all the family that is, and you Bill lad if you want to come," John nodded at Bill as he went on talking,

"So that we can all suggest any new ideas we can come up with to improve the farm income."

"What sort of things Dad? Have you anything in mind?" Howard laid his knife and fork together and pushed his plate away, reaching for his tea cup. His eyes were alight with interest.

"Well your Mum mentioned brown eggs, and Charles' outlet for them. There's a lot of farmers setting up farm shops along the South Coast, to market some of their own produce direct." John suggested.

"Why not here? the Farmer's Weekly had an article about it only last week."

"Yes but we don't have a main road position, surely that would be a must?" Mary asked.

"We have via Charles, if we joined forces." Howard suggested.

"I'm hoping we can all come up with good suggestions, but let's leave it until new year .... we can tell all the family and that will give us all time to come up with fresh ideas. For now we'd better get on with today. These days are so short, it seems to get dark before we can turn round." John led the way towards the door and the yard work waiting outside.

———————————

The next few days brought a fairly rapid thaw to the countryside round Hill Farm. As it became warmer a lot of rain fell, melting and washing away the snow drifts and turning rivers and streams into muddy rapid flowing waterways. Fortunately the wind moved out of the East into the South and an unseasonal but welcome warm breeze blew for a while, day and night. The fields remained damp underfoot but the hill land and the lanes blew dryer than they had been for weeks.

All the farm folk prepared for Christmas. Mary's kitchen was filled with the good smells of cooking. Four Christmas cakes baked with brandy by Mary some weeks before, and kept in sealed tins, were set out on the table. Mary covered them with marzipan and John, who was skilled at the task, iced them and decorated them. Mary finished them with scarlet frills and little trees and snowmen. Jim and Kitty had one, Charles and Gorse had one, Howard and Ling had one. the last one was for Hill Farm for home and need, a little bigger than the others to allow for all the visitors they were expecting to drop in over the festive season. Out of doors Howard fetched trees and holly for all the family. Young Bill did the rounds of the village, keeping up old Granny Radfords tradition with gifts for the less well off. there were baskets of eggs, jars of home-made jam and dressed chickens for old folk on their own and one or two families who had worked for the Radford family in years gone by. Mary and Ling helped decorate the church with holly and ivy and two dozen dark red chrysanthemums from the local nursery. Kitty came over from her lovely garden with variegated holly and a great bundle of winter jasmine, its yellow flowers bursting open in response to the warm wind.

The children all round the family got more and more excited, Gorse told Mary on the phone that Billy, Charles' eldest boy by his first marriage, and now rising eight years old, was just as excited as he had been as a three year old and just as keen to hang up his stocking. For Mary and John the high point of Christmas was just as it had been for many years back, namely the midnight service on Christmas Eve in the old parish church. Howard and Ling were there with little Richard. Sally Anne was at Hill Farm tucked up in John and Mary's big bed, watched over by Billy and his young lady from the village .... a quiet country girl called

Daisy. It was a lovely service, all the old favourite carols with a full Church and Choir to join in. The Church was lit by candle light and hung with holly and evergreens. By the choir stalls stood a big Christmas tree lit all over with white lights. A shining star on the topmost branch. Below the tree a gift from every child in the village school for the local children's home. The school children's crib was below the pulpit lit by a little oil lantern. At the centre of the Church four large advent candles burned low until the church clock struck midnight. At their centre was an unlit even larger candle. At midnight the Rev. Cost put out the four low burning advent candles and lit the tall one at the centre. The Christmas Candle for Christs birth. Rev. Cost then moved across the Church to bless the crib with a prayer, during the singing of the carol Away in a Manger. Later when the congregation was quietly moving up the aisle to take communion, the Choir came down the Church and stood round the tree and sang carols softly until everyone had returned to their seats.

The Carol Service was the most beautiful beginning to Christmas and all the Radfords even the five year old Richard, who was given a blessing at the alter rail kneeling between his Father and Mother, was as quiet as a mouse throughout. His little face was completely absorbed from start to finish.

After Church the family drove home. Mary made hot cocoa, Ling scooped little, fast asleep Sally Anne and wrapped her in a rug provided by Mary. To whispered,

"Goodnight, goodnight, no it's morning now. Happy Christmas, Happy Christmas." All quietly spoken so as not to wake the sleeping little one. John was at the door with the car and quickly took Howard and his little family home to Bunny Warren, then he and Mary went up to bed, tired but full of Christmas Spirit.

"Oh John, how lovely it all is .... all the family at Christmas." Mary settled down into her pillows.

"Aye Lass, and God bless whoever invented electric blankets!" John grinned in the darkness as he moved down between the warm bedclothes.

"It's going colder again tonight I reckon."

"Never mind Dear, all our young ones are well and happy, we can sleep warm and easy until seven, then I shall get up when you do and bring you hot cocoa to the cowsheds, like I used to when we were young." Mary reached over and took his hand under the covers.

"God bless you Darling John. Happy Christmas."

"And you my love, Happy Christmas."

Very soon they were both fast asleep.

Christmas came and went with its round of happy meals at Hill Farm and the other family houses. John and Mary's eldest son Jim brought Kitty, his wife and their two young boys to a cold turkey lunch on Boxing Day. Two days later Kitty gave all the children a party in her huge sitting room. Even little Sally Anne enjoyed the balloons and paper hats and games that followed tea at the long table set with little sandwiches, cakes and biscuits, jellies and ice cream. Gorse and Ling helped with the party, and Mary and John -- everybody's Grand-parents, carted everyone to and fro in the farm car. Howard and Charles stayed home to milk and feed round and generally keep the home-fires burning.

After Christmas as John had predicted it became very cold again with the wind back in the East. Through January there was not very much contact between the families. Jim's energies were taken up coping with keeping their big house warm and to getting to and from work often on dark icebound roads. The two farms kept John, Howard and Charles fully occupied with carrying fodder and bedding to livestock, and with sawing wood to keep the old houses warm. Ling and Mary and Gorse cooked good warming food, dried out wet coats, made up fires and in short gave their menfolk every possible backup in this the most trying month of the year. Mary speaking on the phone to Ling one morning put it all in the nutshell.

"You see Dear the days are so short just now, I'm run off my feet to get breakfast cleared off and get round the poultry and back in time to make a good dinner for twelve noon and kindle a nice fire in the sitting room to warm John through after he's eaten, before he goes back out in the cold again. Then in the afternoon it's a running battle to get the eggs collected and feed round the hens again in time to get tea on in time for after milking. You see they tend to milk a bit earlier because it gets dark so early. Then after tea we no sooner sit down than it's time to put the electric blanket on and make cocoa for bedtime. I've a great pile of mending waiting in the basket, and there are two hundred plus eggs not washed or packed for tomorrow's collection. So that's why I've not walked down to see you."

"You're telling me," Ling resorted to American slang at the other end of the line,

"The moment Howard's gone in the morning, I seem to be thrown in at the deep end with an eternal battle to get the clothes washed, the clothes dried, the clothes ironed and in the drawer before the next mountain of washing needs doing. I try to keep the house warm but Richard wants to be in the garden no matter what the weather and he simply doesn't know the meaning of CLOSE THE DOOR. In summer I wash the clothes and enjoy hanging them in the garden by the orchard where the sun catches them. In no time at all they are ready to fetch in, smelling sweet and dry. At this time of year if I put them out it either rains, snows or the wind blows them away and wraps them round the apple boughs. I finish up with two clothes horses round the stove and fire smuts all over the white undies." Ling paused for breath and then burst on ....

"What do you do at Hill Farm? I know I've got more with

22

two little ones, but John's clothes must get grubby and wet outside. How do you manage?"

"Well as you know, I'm lucky, I've got a line under the hay barn for wet weather, a big airing cupboard, and the Aga is great for wet coats. I'll tell you what I have got, that you could have. One of those old-fashioned airers. They have to be screwed onto the kitchen ceiling and they have four smooth wooden bars passing through four metal supports, one set either end. You let them down on a sort of pulley, load the bars with damp clothes, or ironed clothes needing airing. Then you hoist them up near the ceiling again, out of the way and where the warm air is. I reckon in your kitchen it would work a treat with the heat from your kitchen stove."

"I think I remember one at home when I was small, but it sounds just the ticket for the cottage. Can you spare it?"

"Surely, we never use it now, it's upstairs somewhere decorating the attic. I'll get Howard to bring it down for you. He'll easily carry it. It's not heavy. Must go now and get the eggs washed while I've got a free half-hour." Both women rang off and went back to their labours.

The dark days of January passed by and February came in wet and windy. Two things happened in the early part of February which were both to have an influence on the farm families lives. Both happened before John called his gathering of the clans to discuss and pool ideas for the future. The first of these two events began with a phone call. Mary answered the phone one evening when they were sitting by the fire. The voice on the line she instantly recognised as their nephew, Peter Radford. He was about the same age as Howard and often came to the farm for holidays. The two lads had been great friends as youngsters.

"Hello Peter," said Mary in her kind and welcoming tone,

"How are you? And how's the job and everything?" Peter worked in a local garage near his home in Coventry.

"Well as a matter of fact I'm a bit browned off at the moment .... the garage has folded .... that is it's closed down. It's been hit by the new Coventry bypass scheme and will be demolished in the path of the dual carriageway. They reach our section next week. What's hit us is that we were not told until last week and it hasn't given us much chance to find other jobs. What I wondered, it's a bit of a cheek, but I know Howard always overhauls the farm machinery and tackle in February. Do you think Uncle John would consider letting me come for a month to give Howard a hand in the farm workshop? No pay of course, I've got money put by and I've given up smoking. Just a change of scene and my grub would be great. It would give me the chance to look round for something else. Could you ask him for me?"

Mary detected a bit of anxiety in Peter's request and at once responded in her usual kindly way.

"Of course Dear, but I'm sure you'll be welcome even before I speak to John. Just hold the line a minute." She turned to John who had picked up the gist of the conversation.

"It's Peter John, the garage is closing down, could he come for a month and give Howard a hand with the early Spring machinery clean-up? He says no pay, but we couldn't agree to that could we?" Mary covered the phone with her hand so that Peter would not hear the last words. John grinned at her.

"Tell him to pack his bag and come, we shall be glad to see him and to have his help. We'll discuss money when he gets here but no need to tell him that just now." Mary turned back to the phone.

"John says he will be pleased to have you help and even more pleased to see you. When can you come Love? Tomorrow? I can lay another place at table, easy as catch-a-monkey and make up a bed in Howards old room." Peters spirits obviously lifted at once.

"That's great Aunt Mary, I can catch the ten a.m. and be with you by about twelve-thirty. Don't bother meeting the train. I'll bring my big duffle bag and wear my greatcoat, and come across the fields. Lovely to get out of town and into the fresh air."

"All right Lad, we'll look forward to seeing you tomorrow. Good night now. Good night Dear." Mary came back to the fireside to discuss the unexpected situation with John. Before they went up to bed Mary took a plump chicken out of the freezer to welcome the visitor with a good dinner.

Next morning found Mary busily getting ready for their guest's arrival. She found time to make up the bed in Howard's old room which had a big window facing from the side of the house across the fields and up the hill towards the old mill. She re-lined the drawers with fresh paper and added a comfortable armchair to the furnishings and put out clean towels and a new cake of soap on the hand-basin. Downstairs she rang Ling and invited her to bring the children up to the farm for dinner so that Howard and his family could all be there to welcome Peter. Then they could enjoy a meal altogether.

Peter walked in the door just before twelve-thirty. The men were down the field unblocking an old land drain. Mary welcomed him in as she laid the dinner table.

"Well Peter it's a while since we saw you, could you drink a cup of coffee? The men will be home directly and dinner's on cooking." Mary smiled her welcome. Peter slung his duffle bag to the floor and heaved out of his heavy overcoat.

"I could murder a cup of coffee Aunt Mary, and that dinner smells out of this world. There's never been a kitchen like yours for good smells. It's cooked me walking up the fields .... I'm nearly out of puff. It's gone warmer this morning, no mistake. Was that Uncle John and Howard I saw across the front field as I came up the path? I nearly walked across to them but my pack was too heavy to lug across there.

"Yes they're digging out the old land drain .... it's blocked after last weeks heavy rain."

"My Lord, that drain used to block up years ago when we were little kids. That's what I love most about this place, nothing ever changes."

"What never changes?" Ling's cheerful voice interrupted as she pushed in the pushchair in which Sally Anne was fast asleep.

"Half a sec, don't answer that, I'll pop the pushchair in the front room. Sally Anne will likely sleep until after dinner if we let her." Ling suited the action to the words and took the sleeping child through to the far room. Young Richard came into the house and shyly stood by Mary, trying to think where he had seen the man with the blue eyes and fair curly hair before. But anyway as the blue eyes met the brown eyes in the questioning face of the five year old a friendship was born and both smiled at each other.

"You've grown up a bit son. Last time I came you were the one in the pushchair, now you are nearly grown-up." Peter leaned over and ruffled Richard's dark hair as he spoke.

"This is your Dad's old friend and cousin, Peter .... do you remember him?" Mary asked.

"Yes I think I just do, but I'm not really grown-up yet. I'm not quite five. I start in school at Easter, Mummy says." Richard answered gravely.

"But I can nearly read, Mummy is showing me how. Sally Anne can't, she's only a baby really and of course she's only a girl."

"Ah yes of course that makes all the difference, we men must stick together, I've always found that." Peter grinned broadly as he spoke. Any more conversation was interrupted because John and Howard came in through the door, ready for their dinner. Mary left them all to talk and made the coffee for Peter to stand and drink while they all exchanged news. Presently Howard carried Peter's bag upstairs followed by Peter and little Richard who proudly showed Peter his room and the bathroom next door.

"Have you come here to live Uncle Peter .... that would be spiffing? We had a lot of snow you know. I'm hoping we'll have some more and ice on the pond. Nanny doesn't want any more, she says she can't do with it because it gets underfoot. I don't understand that .... do you know? I mean how can it get underfoot when it is already underfoot?"

"Well you know how it is with ladies. Ladies know a lot that we don't, but if Aunt Mary says so then it must be so." Peter and Howard's deep voiced laughter could be heard by those in the kitchen as they came back downstairs. A happy meal was enjoyed by everyone. Mary and Ling had a chat about Ling's new airer which Howard had put up for her and which was proving a godsend in the cottage kitchen. The three men discussed farm affairs, the rising price of feed stuffs, and the lack of rise in milk prices at the farm gate and the worrying effect of these two facts on farmers. Mary served them a delicious lunch. Chicken with stuffing, roast and mashed potatoes, peas and carrots. This was followed by treacle steam pudding with a jug of custard and Jersey cream from home.

After dinner the three men went out to see to the stock and outside jobs. Mary and Ling washed up together and gave Sally Anne her dinner in the high-chair kept at Hill Farm just for that purpose. Then Ling collected Richard from outside and set off for home wheeling the pushchair.

"Love to stay longer, but need to get tea on for Howard and bring in coal and logs while the light lasts. It still goes so cold in the evenings and I like to keep a good fire. Thanks again Mum for the airer it's really made my work easier. No washing underfoot and it dries in half the time up in the warm air near the ceiling."

"That's fine Lass, see you soon, Winter's nearly gone and when the days get longer we'll be able to see more of each other." Mary waved goodbye and saw them off down the yard before going down the orchard to see to the poultry.

The other event which was to affect the farm folks lives and which happened in February, was actually a two-part happening and was in the first place more to do with Howard and Ling than with Hill Farm itself.

STRAWBERRIES AND CREAM

Chapter 3

The Windfall

STRAWBERRIES AND CREAM

Chapter 3

The Windfall

On February the fourteenth Ling came downstairs a few minutes after Howard had called his usual goodbye and gone across the fields to milk the cows. Ling busied herself getting the children dressed and putting their breakfast in front of them. Soon they were all sitting at table eating hot creamy porridge. Ling spooned into Sally Anne's mouth between enjoying eating her own. There came a double tap on the door.

"Posty-man, you get it Richard Love." Richard wriggled his behind off his stool, dropped to the floor and ran to tug the door open.

"Morning Postman," called Ling.

"Morning Lass, morning youngster, two for your Mam today. One's come from a long way across the water. Over the sea; look them stamps is from Canada .... T'other side of the world you know." He grinned down at Richard and was gone.

"Thank you Postman," called Ling after his retreating back, as she took the two letters from Richard.

"Can we open them Mummy?" Richard stood hopefully by the table.

"You get back on your stool Love and finish your porridge, I can open this one, but the one from Canada is Daddy's. He'll have to open it at dinner time. It's most likely from his Aunt, she lives out there, although .... " Ling frowned as she spoke, "it's typed and not in Aunt Maggie's writing. Never mind, put it on the sitting room mantle-shelf. Dad will see it. Let's open this one. Oh how lovely it's a Valentine card from Daddy, and look it's got two rabbits on the front."

"What is it for .... it's not your birthday is it Mummy?"

Richard asked seriously.

"No, no it's not my birthday, it just means that Daddy loves me very much, and I love him too, we all do don't we my chicken?"

"Oh yes Daddy's the very bestest Daddy, isn't he?" Richard's brown eyes glowed as he spoke. They both enjoyed the Valentine card and completely forgot the long white envelope from Canada.

Dinner time came and went. Howard and Ling enjoyed shepherd's pie and peas in the kitchen at the cottage. Both children enjoyed their dinners and sat at table good as gold. This gave their parents the chance to talk.

"You know Dad wants us all to have a get-together and think up some ideas to improve the farm income? Well Charles' farm as well if possible?" Howard finished his jam tart and custard and glanced across the table at her as he spoke.

"Yes I've been thinking about it. I'd love a finger in the farm pie, but I'm not sure how." Ling replied.

"Well," Ling knew at once by Howard's face that something interesting was coming.

"Well, I heard something interesting in the village when I went to the Post Office to fetch Dad's paper." Howard had always had the knack of getting hold of titbits of local gossip before anyone else in the family.

"Whatever was it?" Ling's face was a picture of curiosity.

"Manor Farm, on the green at Brushstoke, just across the reservoir. Well it's coming on the market .... first time for a hundred years. There's eighty acres, the Manor House and a set of buildings." Howard paused and sat looking at her keenly for several minutes.

"But Howard, what's in that for us? It can't .... you can't mean that Dad might buy it and put both farms together. Surely we couldn't possibly afford it? What does your Dad say?" Howard grinned and said nothing.

"Oh Howard, you haven't even told him yet. However did you manage? If I'd known it would have burst out of me the minute I saw any of the family."

"I hope not, I want to keep it dark for a few days while I think it over and make a few enquiries. D'you remember how my Mum bought this cottage for us and kept it secret, hoping we would get engaged .... and then we did. Well I can't help thinking that if Dad's on 'Big is beautiful' and all that, and Mum and Gorse and you are interested in the idea of a farm shop and there's eighty acres adjoining our own land with a lovely old house right on a village green, with a main road position. Well I ask you isn't it tempting? Of course as you say money's going to be the problem .... we haven't got much. Dad and Mum couldn't run another farm. Old Charles is only just starting in a farm. The only possibility is would they rent it to us as we are neighbours, or maybe give us a big mortgage? Of course I know that Dad'd be dead against that last idea and it would be a millstone round our necks." Howard paused and looked at his wife, a question in his eyes.

"Oh Howard I know exactly what's going through your head, ever since you heard in the Post Office, but I just can't see how we could possibly manage it. It would put a huge burden on us all and I think Dad is thinking of the children .... I mean six lads in the family who may want to come on the farm one day .... only Sally Anne to set them off. Mary says Radford men only have one pattern." Ling laughed but there was a trace of tears in her voice. She was so afraid that Howard was going to be terribly disappointed.

"Now my Love don't put me off first go, I've only known for two and a half hours, give me time to find out about this and just keep it under your hat for the moment. Anyway I must get back, we're building a new lambing area with hurdles and separate cubicles this afternoon and I'm nearly on the hour already."

"We'll talk about it this evening, by the fire, maybe we can think of something." Ling reached up to kiss him, giving him a hug at the same time.

"Bye Love, see you soon." and he was gone.

All afternoon Ling racked her brains to recall every detail she could remember about Manor Farm. She had walked across some of it's fields with Howard by footpath to have a drink at the old pub on the green at Brushstoke when they were engaged. The pub, called the Plough, was a much loved local in the area. She remembered the Manor House opposite as being behind a low wall with a garden area in front. A path leading to the door. She thought the house had long low windows downstairs at the front and that the roof above had two peaks with a window in each facing across the road. To the right of the house there was a wide farm-gate entrance leading into a large farmyard. Round the yard she remembered a set of buildings including a big barn. More than that she could not remember. She turned to thinking of Howard. He seemed so keen on this, was he going to be upset when it proved to be beyond anyone's means? In the end she put it out of her mind and concentrated on her ordinary afternoons work. It wasn't until she went, armed with sticks and firelighter, to kindle the sitting room fire, that she saw the envelope on the mantle-shelf and realised that she had completely forgotten about it at dinner time.

"Oh well, it may cheer Howard up to have a letter waiting for him when he gets back. A nice supper and a letter. That can't be bad." Howard was back in good time that evening. The farm was gradually drying out, and the work getting easier. Peter was proving a great help. At many of the farm tasks he was not yet skilled, but he was unfailingly cheerful and would have a try at anything. Howard had noticed that his Father had looked less tired since Peter's coming. Mary, who missed nothing had noticed it too. She put it down in part to the physical help Peter was giving John, but also in part to the pleasure of having a youngster in the house again. Mary was so pleased that she was determined to try to find a way for Peter to stay on after the end of February. Also Mary liked to see Howard get home earlier some evenings to spend time with Ling and the children.

This was one of those evenings, and Howard came in in time to tuck up Richard in his little bed, and kiss Sally Anne, who was fast asleep in her cot. Howard enjoyed a quick wash and changed into flannels and a clean shirt, and came down to supper. There was a lovely fire in the sitting room, and his old slippers by the hearth. Ling's voice came from the kitchen.

"Sit down I know you're tired, I've got eggs on toast ready, just got to make the tea then I'll bring the tray through. By the way there's a letter for you on the shelf from Canada I think."

"So there is I'll read it after supper, doesn't look like my Aunt, it's typed."

"That's what I thought," said Ling coming through the door with the tray. Howard lifted the coffee table in front of the fire, and they both sat down to enjoy the food. After the meal Ling stretched out her legs to the blaze and lay back in the big armchair.

"Oh lovely," she sighed, "a bit of quiet by the fireside." She closed her eyes and dozed. Howard reached up to the shelf and took his letter. He slit it open with a knife and drew out two sheets of headed notepaper. He read them through quietly. Ling drifted into a light sleep. On the mantle the clock ticked. The cat purred on the hearth rug. Howard read the two sheets of paper through twice and folding them neatly returned them to the envelope. He got up quietly and going across to the little desk in the window he unlocked a small drawer, placed the envelope inside, re-locked the drawer again and slipped the key into his pocket. Sitting down again he bent over the tea tray and poured out two cups of tea. He woke Ling gently by tickling her foot.

"Wake up Lovebird, cup of tea?" She opened her eyes and smiled.

"Only dozed for a minute, it's the warmth of the fire. bought any nice farms lately Lover-boy?"

"Not yet, I haven't been to see it you see, can't decide anything until I've seen it can I?" His eyes glowed at her and his slow smile warmed her.

"You're not really going to see it are you? Not without telling Dad?"

"I'm certainly not telling Dad or anyone yet. We shall see what we shall see shan't we my Love?"

"If you sit there grinning like a Cheshire Cat, I shall thump you Howard Radford. Do you know something I don't or something?"

"A great many things no doubt, but then I'm older than you are little Linglet. People always grow wiser as they get older." He was still smiling at her as he spoke. Soon afterwards they cleared away the tray, washed up, put the guard on the fire and went to bed. Outside the night was mild, under the garden hedge the field-mouse moved a little in his Winter sleep. On the hill the grass roots began to move in the soil. Spring was on the way.

———————————

Next morning Howard and John were in the cowsheds. It was Peter's day to have the extra hour in bed. When the last of the cows had been milked Howard asked John casually if he could have a few hours off that morning, on the grounds that he wanted to get into Banworth to buy a surprise for Ling. Howard rarely asked for time off and John at once agreed.

"Never feel you've got to ask Lad. We all work hard here and any one of us is entitled to an hour or two .... especially when we're in a slack period like now. Another thing, with Peter here it has lightened the load on all the rest of us. I wonder if he'd stop longer? Until after lambing say. D'you think he would?"

"You'd have to ask him Dad, I think he might, but can we afford it?"

"Well, he won't take much money. your Mother and I have both tried to persuade him. I think the budget would stand it. The cows are doing well and we do get the Jersey high butterfat premium. It's the cost of the feed we've got to watch, perhaps grow more of our own another year. But another thing is your Mother's poultry are laying a treat and she has already offered to help with money towards Peter stopping on, if we can get him to think about it. Anyhow let's get our breakfast, here comes Peter now, we can discuss it later."

Soon after breakfast Howard took the car and went home to change. Ling knew he was up to something the moment he came in the door. He was not to be drawn however and insisted that he was going in to Banworth on a quick errand for John.

"Well I believe you, but thousands wouldn't." said Ling unconvinced. "There's a clean shirt in the drawer and your brown shoes are in the shoe rack." She grinned up at him and went on with the children's washing.

On his way upstairs he collected the letter he had locked in the drawer and slipped it into his jacket pocket, thanking his lucky stars that Ling seemed to have forgotten all about it. Fifteen minutes later he was in the car heading for Banworth. When he reached the town centre he parked the car at the back of the Swan public house before making his way along the street. The first person he bumped into was his brother Charles.

"Hello there, have we both managed to escape for an hour then?" Charles greeted him.

"Yes I've got one or two calls to make, you haven't by any chance got your Land-Rover here have you?"

"Yes I'm picking up two bags of poultry feed, and I'm going out to Hill Farm to take some tools back to Dad, can I transport something for you?" Charles asked. Howard looked at the kindly reliable face before him. In childhood he had been closer to his elder brother Jim and Charles the middle brother had been a bit of an odd man out. But since Charles had left industry and bought a farm, his parents and Howard had come to value his kind nature and got to know him as a man in a way none of them had known him as a boy. He was of medium height and firm build. His green eyes were the same colour as Howard's but there the resemblance ended. Howard was tall and dark with wavy hair and strong features. Charles had brown curly hair and neat regular features. His whole bearing was compact and neat. He was always ready to help anyone anywhere and doing so was obviously a pleasure to him. As now, when his face lit, when Howard replied saying,

"I'm hoping to buy Ling a special gift, a twin-tub washing

machine actually, but I have another call to make first. Are you going elsewhere?"

"Yes groceries for Gorse and the vets as well. Could we have a coffee after?" Charles pointed towards the little tea shop along the street.

"Yes fine, let's meet up there in three quarters of an hour or so."

"Fine it is, I'll see you there, I'll push on now."

They went their ways and Howard went up the steps into the office of Renards solicitors and a moment later was shaking hands with Dick Warren the Radford's family solicitor. After greetings had been exchanged, Dick indicated a chair and sat down behind his desk.

"Well now, what can I do for you Howard?" The bright eyes in the keen face were intent and a trifle disconcerting. Howard took the long white envelope from Canada out of his pocket and handed it across the desk without speaking. Dick Warren looked carefully at the letter heading and then slowly read the contents. After a few minutes he spoke.

"Is this man Howard Letts anything to do with you Howard, I notice he has the same christian names?"

"Yes he is, or was, my uncle by marriage. He married my Mother's sister and took her off to Canada very much against the families wishes I gather. It was before I was born. Later he deserted my Aunt and left her with two little daughters. I just about remember him sending me a birthday card as a small child."

"Ah, so he knew you were named for him .... perhaps that accounts for it."

"Well when I read the letter, that's what I wondered, but the thing is, do you think it's genuine? Also if it is, what does it amount to?"

"It looks genuine to me, but I can check for you in five minutes on the phone, and what it amounts to. Want me to try?" Dick Warren was smiling broadly now.

"Yes please, but don't worry, I haven't told a soul in case it's not genuine."

"Well let's see, it'll take a few minutes to get through I dare say." Dick Warren picked up the phone, spread the letter before him, and dialled the operator. After what seemed to Howard an age, but was in fact only a few minutes, he began to speak to the firm in Canada who had sent the letter. From then on Dick was mostly on the listening end of the conversation, with only a few 'Yes.' 'Oh yes I see.' 'Oh good' and the like until he said,

"And what is the rate of exchange for English Pounds. Oh yes, and what about identification at this end? Ah yes, I can certainly do that. What about Mr. Letts own family in Canada? How do they stand? I see, provided for. This is a separate bequest. Right thank you, that's all I need to know. I'll tell my client and send the necessary paperwork." Dick Warren put down the phone, rested his arms on the desk, and sat with the tips of his fingers resting together in front of him. A smile spread across his face.

"There we are then Howard, all quite above board. Your Uncle in Canada has left you 16,000 Canadian Dollars. He was a wealthy man when he died six weeks ago. His wife and daughters are well provided for." Howard drew in a deep breath.

"How much .... how much is 16,000 dollars in English money?"

"About £10,500."

"I simply can't believe it, it's an absolute fortune."

"I'm sure that it is true, have you really kept it a secret, even from Ling?"

"Yes I couldn't bear her to be disappointed." Howard looked absolutely knocked out as he smiled somewhat shamefaced across the desk.

"Well go along and tell her now, I've another client due shortly. Leave the letter with me, I'll sort it all out for you this end." Dick rose to his feet as he spoke.

"Oh of course, and thank you so much Dick, never fail the Radfords do you? Much appreciated in this case I can tell you."

A few minutes later Howard was in the shop choosing a twin-tub washing machine for Ling, after a quick dive into the bank to line his pocket with enough money for his purchase. Next he belted along to the Estate Agents, where he collected the particulars of Manor Farm, Brushstoke, and the key to the back door of the farmhouse. He spoke for a few minutes to the senior partner who was in his office. Then Howard rushed off down the street to reach the table for two in the coffee shop five minutes behind Charles. He felt dazed and somewhat shaken.

"Are you all right, did you get it?"

"What, get what?" Howard felt he was pulling himself back from somewhere far off.

"A twin-tub for Ling. Did you get it?" Charles looked quite worried. "Here's your coffee, put some sugar in it and get it down you." he advised.

"Oh yes, yes I did, I said we'd pick it up in a few minutes, it's very good of you to transport it home for us Charles."

Both men drank their coffee, and Charles brought the conversation round to farming. Howard slipped easily into the talk. After they finished their coffee, for which Charles insisted on paying, they went to the car park and collected the Land-Rover. The shop helped load the washing machine, and Charles set off for the farm. Howard felt that he walked on air as he went back to his car. He spent the journey forcing himself back to calmness, he wanted to keep secret a little longer.

———————

Ling was so thrilled with the twin-tub that she could hardly speak.

"Oh Howard how lovely, but I'm sure you can't really afford it."

"Yes I can, it was the last of the January Sale this week, so I got quite a bit off. Mum and I both feel that with two little ones, and dirty farm clothes from me as well, you need all the help you can get with the washing Lovelet."

"You're a lovely lovely man, and I'm so glad to have married you."

"Well of course I agree with that entirely." Howard lay back in his chair and watched her under his lashes. They both laughed into each others eyes. Their bond of love strong as ever, and they totally happy within it's prison.

———————

Two days later it was Howard's Sunday off. Since Peter's coming, all three men had been able to have one Sunday off in three and still leave two to do the milking in good time. Mary and Ling found their menfolk more relaxed in the pleasure of looking forward to a bit of free time. This particular Sunday, it was fine and there was more than a hint of Spring in the air. At breakfast time Ling said

"What shall we do today, are we going to Church?"

"No I'm taking you for a ride in the car, I've arranged it with Dad, he and Mum are having both the nippers. I'll take them along after breakfast if you could wash up and put your jacket on. I'll bring the car back."

"You're a dark horse, arranging all this on the Q.T., I shall want to change into something pretty you know. Are we going out to lunch?"

"Well, we are and we aren't. I'd rather you stay as you are really."

"What, in these old slacks?" Ling's eyebrows flew up.

"Yes, very nice, very suitable, bring your wellies too." Howard grinned at her.

"Are we going to nanny's house?" Young Richard never missed a trick.

"Yes you are, nip and get your coat." Howard lifted Sally Anne out of the high-chair, sponged her mouth and hands and pulled on her coat and leggings. A moment later he set off up the lane pushing the pushchair with Richard running on ahead. Ling waved them off and then hurried up with clearing the table and washing the pots. Ten minutes later Howard was back with the car.

"Come on Love, it's quite a nice day, just the job." He picked up both their pairs of wellingtons and threw them into the car boot. They drove off along the lane into the Banworth road. A few minutes later they had followed the main road round the shoulder of the hill and through the village and on in the general direction of Coventry. Suddenly Ling realised where they were going.

"We're going to see that farm, Manor Farm, aren't we Howard?"

"Yes, yes we are. I just would like us to have seen it." He finished on a rather lame note.

"Well I shall love to see it, especially the house, I believe the Darren family have lived there as long as anyone can remember, I've certainly never been in the house."

"Granny used to visit there for bridge parties I think, but it must be at least eighteen years ago."

"Well I shall enjoy going round but I shall try my hardest not to get too much in love with anything, because I'm certain it will be far beyond our means. So don't worry about me Howard."

"I never worry about you Love, you are always such a cheerful little bird, no matter what hits us." Howard turned the car into the main road, beyond the railway bridge heading for Brushstoke.

"Do keep your feet on the ground too Darling, I'm so sure we can't afford it, I don't want you to be hurt." Ling sounded a bit anxious. Howard made a face at her, and then at himself in the driving mirror before he replied.

"I promise to keep the money side in mind all the time I'm there." He said at last.

"Here we are now, could you open the yard gate? I'd rather park in the yard than on the main road." They had pulled up in the middle of Brushstoke village. The village green was on the right, with the Plough pub beyond, and old cottages ranged round the green together with the Post Office come shop. Further on they could see more cottages, a small council estate and the Parish Hall surrounded by oak trees. Then on the other side of the main road stood the Police house, a track which led to the Water Works building, by the reservoir, several more cottages and the Manor Farm house, they had come to look at. They drew into the gateway alongside and Ling climbed out to open the gate which led into the farmyard beyond. Ling walked in after the car. She saw that the house stood back from the road as she had remembered, with an area of walled garden in front. Through the farm gate they went along the side of the house and she could see an extension at the back with windows facing the farmyard, which was surrounded by buildings some of which screened it from the busy main road. Ling walked in after the car and when Howard drew to a halt and stopped the engine she was at once conscious of a sort of quiet orderly peace. The old red-brick buildings were neat painted and tidy and although so close to the main road, they muffled out the traffic's noise. In front of Ling was a length of brick paved yard which led on alongside the back garden wall and thence to a field gate. Beyond the gate Ling could see several big oak trees and a glimpse through their bare branches of the reservoir and more fields over to the right and left.

Howard got out of the car, and came to join her.

"How quiet it is in here, off the main road, and look there's a gate to the fields. Let's put our wellies on and then go that way first." Soon they were going through the field gate. They found themselves in a pasture field. Behind the buildings, enclosed by a low brick wall was a Dutch barn. It was nearly full of hay and straw.

"Must have got the hay and corn harvest, after they finished with stock, probably why the yard's so tidy." Howard's farmers eye had come to the fore.

"This is a lovely field and the next one to it, just a few oaks in the hedges, and a little mound with trees on the top." Ling's

43

quick eyes looked about her.

"Looks like an ancient burial ground, let's look." Howard strode off towards the tiny hill and Ling ran to keep up with him. Soon they had climbed the mound and found they could see in all directions. Back towards the house and buildings, which looked as though they had been there since time began, they could see the garden wall and the lawn beyond. A nut bush dangling with early catkins was in the garden and beneath its boughs a carpet of yellow aconites and clumps of snowdrops.

Looking to the East and West they could see fields, level and all under cultivation. some were ploughed, but not sown, and some were pasture. the two fields close to the house had a slight slope up towards the reservoir and were both grass. The mound they stood on was in the larger of these two fields. The best and most interesting view from here however was due North. A grassy bank sloped gently up to the reservoir. Then the lovely stretch of water with small areas of woodland on the far bank. Ducks and a pair of swans could be seen on the water. Beyond the water the familiar slope of grass fields up to Hill Farm and home. The railway and brook between the reservoir and Hill Farm could not be seen from here. The trees and hedgerows hid them from view. On the brow of the hill the homely outline of Hill Farm house, the silver birch in Mary's garden, now just a tracery of black branches above the silver trunks. The wide spreading oak tree and the apple and damson trees in the orchard. And not least the line of old trees along the lane to the left of the new cubicle housing and the parlour and the old cowsheds. It was a view to delight them both.

"It looks far nearer from this side." Ling stood drinking in the greeny-browns of the Winter scene in the pale sunlight of the February afternoon.

"How do you mean? we never look at it this way on as a rule. We look across here." Howard pointed out.

"Yes I know, but when you are over there, over here looks quite far off. I think what I really mean is that I had no idea that this farm was so near. Why the fields adjoin us except for the railway line."

"I know, that's why I was so interested, and the tunnel under the railway where the footpath comes through is big enough for a tractor and tackle, but not unfortunately big enough for loads of hay and straw."

"Howard you've thought it all out haven't you?"

"Well I've certainly mulled it around in my head. Big loads would have to go over the level crossing."

"Where is the level crossing, not on our land is it?"

"No it's just off our land, along by Brushstoke station. That's nearly into Ferry End village." Brushstoke Church, Vicarage and station and also the school were two miles further up the road. The Manor Farm, the Plough and the village green formed almost a separate village.

"There's a foredrift, a sort of green lane from the level crossing by the station which leads onto the bottom corner of our Caravan field."

"I remember seeing it when we've worked down there." Ling replied, thinking back in her mind to harvest time.

"Let's go back and look at the buildings and inside the house." Howard suggested.

"Have you got the key? Oh Howard you have been a dark horse over this. When do you intend telling your Mum and Dad?"

"Tomorrow I should think. I'm hoping Dad will have this family get together he's been on about since Christmas. Then you and Mum and all of us could pool any ideas we have for upping the farm incomes a bit. We certainly need to grow more of our own cattle feed than we do. These fields would give us enough land to be able to do that. Also the main road position we'd need if we thought about a farm shop. A lot of people use this main road for Tamworth and Coventry. We could have nice painted signs outside."

"Howard, d'you think we really could? Perhaps there would be room for a tearoom in the house. Your Mum and I would love a tearoom." Ling's enthusiasm bubbled up as she spoke.

"Now you're getting as bad as me, I thought you said don't fall in love with the place." But Howard was laughing as he spoke.

"Yes but that's easy as pie when you haven't seen any of it. When you see these lovely fields, so near our own, and these buildings, in such good repair and neat painted." She stopped speaking as they came back into the yard and Howard reached to open the first pen door. Inside was a long old-style cowshed with thirty two standings, this led into the old cooling house still with washing up trough and taps. Beyond were calf pens and granary with loft over, open fronted implement sheds and on the other side of the yard a range of old stables where the cart horses must have been housed. Again there was a loft overhead, also on that side was a harness room. Beyond was a large barn with a door close by leading to a short concrete yard with four pigsties and a folding area for sheep. Beyond the yard was an orchard with perhaps a dozen young apple trees carefully spaced and pruned.

"Just an unspoiled set of old buildings, but they could be adapted to all sorts of present day uses," Howard didn't miss a detail as he looked around. "And all the doors and windows are in such good condition, and the roofs. Even the pigsties and little back places. Someone has really cared for this place."

They went back into the large farmyard and across to the little gate in the wall which led to the back door of the farmhouse. Howard pulled the big old key from his pocket and fitted it into the lock. It turned smoothly and the door opened into a big long kitchen with white painted windows on three sides of the room. The walls were also painted white. The whole effect of the room was of light and air. There was a very modern stainless steel sink unit under one window a very heavy long old pine table with drawers either end, down the middle of the room. The floor was of six inch square red quarry tiles. Everywhere was very clean. the rest of the house was the same. There were two large front sitting rooms facing across the garden to the Plough pub. Both these rooms had wide ingle-nook fireplaces and exposed beams. There was a smaller sitting room behind with a field view and

46

another little room which had obviously been an office. At the back near the kitchen was a small newly fitted downstairs toilet with a hand-basin in the corner. There were also two large pantrys in this area and a door leading into the rear garden.

In front of the house a wide hallway separated the two front sitting rooms. From here a wide oak staircase led up to the first floor. The stairs were still covered in a deep pile old fashioned red patterned carpet. Upstairs there were five bedrooms and a bathroom, and a separate toilet. The two front bedrooms had fitted hand-basins. They wandered from room to room.

"It all seems so well-cared for, in such good order as though the family had only left yesterday." Ling sat on the top step of the stairs, fingering the carpet. "Do you know how long ago they left?"

"No idea, I don't even know why they left. Come on Love, it gets dark early, the sun will soon be gone, let's get back to tea."

"All right, let me just peep at the back garden, I want to see the snowdrops." Ling pulled the bolts on the back door to the garden, and a moment later they were on the garden path. The snowdrops and aconites were not the only flowers out, a winter jasmine on the wall of the house was also in flower. Ling looked at the long arching sprays of golden flowers, the buds tipped with red before they came fully open.

"It's lovely isn't it, you can see the attic windows and the chimneys of Hill Farm from here, look through the trees. She pointed across the fields beyond the low garden wall.

Soon they were driving home. Howard took the car straight to Hill Farm where they collected the children. John was about to start milking. Peter was already across in the milk parlour. Mary was pouring the inevitable cup of tea. Young Richard was jumping up and down telling all his adventures.

"I picked all the eggs from under the hens, and they was all warm in the feathers, and my Nanny putted them in the basket and I never dropped none. And we had chocolate biscuits after dinner. And the man in the white dress at the Church said he once Christed me and I had growed and growed." Richard stopped for want of breath and Sally Anne sat smiling in her pushchair.

"As you've heard we've had a lovely day." Mary said smiling fondly on the two little ones. "Have you enjoyed your day, did you go far?"

"Yes we went to look at Manor Farm, Brushstoke, it's just come on the market." Howard grinned, delighting in their amazed faces.

"D'you mean across the water here .... never .... they've been there longer than we've been here." John looked staggered.

"How did you find out about that Howard? I've never known anyone who could sniff out news like you can, except p'raps Granny Radford, she always heard every morsel before anyone else got so much as a sniff." Mary was laughing as she spoke.

"It's not only that Mum, he's on to adding it to Hill Farm and having a farm shop and tearoom to say nothing of 'Pick Your Own Strawberries'," Ling burst out.

"Who the devil said anything about strawberries? I never said a damn thing about strawberries." Yelled Howard indignantly.

"Well it was only a matter of time before you thought of it, so I thought I'd put one over on you for a change. I'm not just a pretty face you know." Ling looked into Howard's face her own dead serious, but she couldn't keep it up and almost at once burst out laughing.

"And did young Howard by any chance suggest what we should use for money?" John asked, only half-joking.

"Never a word, I told him he was in cloud cuckoo land, but it was fun to see it just the same." Ling smiled lovingly as she spoke, her eyes on Howard's cheerful face.

"I think you should call in all the lot of us and have that family gathering you were talking about at Christmas. Pool our ideas and discuss the farms; Charles' farm as well as ours. And that place across the water as well while we're about it, after all you never know .... well do you?"

"No lad you're right, you never do know, not to be certain that is. Anyway I'll get on the blower to Jim and Charles and

48

we'll have a party. What about that then Mary Love? Good excuse for a party don't you think?"

"Lovely Dear, a supper party, buffet, everyone help themselves, and a real family discussion after. How about next Sunday night? It's your Sunday on, but you could all share the milking and be done early. All us women could get the eats ready and get the children to bed if necessary. That would be lovely for a start!" Mary was smiling and her eyes twinkled behind her specs.

"I'll have to get milking now or Peter 'll think I've left him to it." John moved towards the door pausing to add as he went out

"And I think Peter should be in on the discussion, he's family, and he might be persuaded to stay on, which Mary and I are both in favour of."

"So are we Dad, he's been a real help since he came but what he needs is a wife to keep his feet on Hill Farm soil." Howard helped Richard, who had been listening spellbound for the last few minutes, to put his coat on. Ling caught hold of the pushchair handles and a few minutes later Howard and his family were on the way down the lane heading for home.

"It was dusk now and they were glad to get into the warmth of the cottage kitchen. In bed later that night, Ling whispered to Howard.

"Well anyway even if nothing can come of it we had a lovely day. I wouldn't have missed seeing Manor Farm for the world."

"I know Love, but do you realise that in all the excitement of the fields and the house and everything, we never had any lunch? I was going to treat us at the Plough, but it went right out of my head."

"Why do you think I made that huge fry-up for our supper when we got back? I was afraid we might starve else. Next time we go on an adventure I'm going to take a packed lunch of ham sandwiches, just in case."

A few minutes later they were both fast asleep.

STRAWBERRIES AND CREAM

Chapter 4

Family Gathering

STRAWBERRIES AND CREAM

Chapter 4

Family Gathering

The next week soon passed by and on the Sunday evening the four women, Mary, Ling, Gorse and Kitty, who had been busy cooking each in their own kitchens all weekend, were setting out a tasty buffet supper, on Hill Farms big kitchen table. On the white cloth plates of sandwiches, crisp topped quiches, sausage rolls, cheese straws, pork pies, cold sausages on sticks were the savouries. Chocolate eclairs, a large trifle and one of Mary's big fruit cakes were the sweets. With any spaces filled up with baskets of rolls and dishes of home-made butter patted into shape with Mary's old wooden butter pats. Gorse had made and brought with her a big glass dish of green salad with hard-boiled eggs on top. It made a colourful sight in the middle of the table. The whole table was a good welcome for the menfolk who had all gone to help with feeding round and milking. Only Charles had not come yet. He had brought Gorse over earlier with her food for the party and gone back to see to his own milking and stock. He was expected back anytime.

Upstairs almost every bed was full. All the children had vastly enjoyed the fun of all of them going to bed in Nanny's house. At first excitement had kept them awake, but Ling and Gorse had settled them down and now all the little ones were sound asleep. Gorse's twin boys aged two ended up in Peter's bed, side by side with Billy in a camp-bed alongside to give them a bit of security. Sally Anne was well used to John and Mary's big bed, and a bolster down the middle gave Richard his share. Kitty's two older boys, Simon and Nicky, were in a single bed in the spare room and were lucky, as being older they had a portable TV to watch and the promise of a tray of goodies to be

53

smuggled up by Kitty later on.

All the men were in the house and changed and ready for supper by seven o'clock. Charles was the last to arrive having had to travel from River Farm after milking. When he came in the door everyone else was gathered in the kitchen ready to enjoy the buffet as soon as he arrived. Seeing him coming in the door looking his usual quiet shy self Gorse slipped through the family ranks filling the kitchen with chat and laughter and taking his hand drew him into a corner near the Aga.

"I'm so glad you're here." Her elfin face lit up as she spoke, "I felt lost with all the others here except you."

"What a spread, if we demolish all that lot we shall all burst." Charles laid his arm across her shoulders catching his Mother's welcoming eyes upon him as he spoke.

"Now then everybody, it's help yourselves tonight. Plates are piled either end so choose what you want and take it through to the sitting room. Peter and Bill are here as family tonight, so make them welcome." Mary set everyone a good example by stopping speaking and picking up a plate. Soon all present were talking and laughing and eating. Most of the conversation was, as usual amongst farmers, concerned with livestock and crops, the state of the markets and the weather. Even Jim and Kitty, sitting side by side on the settee, were discussing Market Gardening with Ling and Howard. Mary looked round the room and listened to the rise and fall of the voices and the occasional bursts of laughter, often from Howard and Peter, who seemed to be in good humour. Mary's eyes were full of joy, that special joy she always felt when all the family were gathered together.

"Just your cup of tea eh Love?" John winked at her and patted her arm.

"It's so nice to see them all together, we hardly ever manage it. And all the children under our roof. Oh John I could almost cry with the pleasure of it."

"Now then Lass, none of that it's a party remember." John lifted his hand and touched her cheek.

Presently everyone had finished eating, plates were stacked in the sink and food remains put on the pantry shelves. When everyone was seated, all eyes turned to John, quietly lighting his pipe in his fireside chair.

"Well Dad, fire away, give us a general lead then we can all have a say, to see what the combined Radford brains can come up with." Jim grinned round the group as he spoke. John laid aside his pipe and turned to face them all.

"Well it's like this, I have, and your Mother too of course, been so happy and glad to welcome all our grandchildren. No grandparents ever had lovelier grandchildren. Of course, we'd not have minded a few more of the other pattern, but hopefully Sally Anne is only a beginning." General laughter followed this. "But I feel we all need to think about this new generation of Radfords growing up. We are sure to have some of the children wanting to farm. It is up to us to prepare for that now, see the way ahead and make the farms as good and as productive as we can. The farm papers all point towards sidelines. In the fifties it was easier. Even in the early sixties, but we have to realise that the sixties are passing and stock-feed prices are rising all the time. Here at Hill Farm we ought to be growing more feed for our own animals. Barley and oats and perhaps roots as well. What I'm thinking is that if we all pool our ideas. Howard I know has some thoughts on the subject, but we'd also like to hear from all the rest of you. Come on Charles you're on a low acreage compared with what the powers that be consider to be a viable unit; dreadful expression that; but do you think your acres will feed and provide a living for your family in the years ahead?" John looked across at Charles as he spoke. Charles smiled quietly.

"I've got to say it does worry me at times, my acres won't support more milking cows, I think small farms will eventually be squeezed out unless they diversify. Our farm gate sales of eggs are very good and rising all the time. Gorse has expanded the poultry a lot this last year. We are doing dressed poultry to order now as well, and that too is expanding. I think that long term farms will have to specialise in one or two things and do them really well." Charles stopped speaking and looked round the room.

"Something like calf rearing perhaps?" This from Howard.

"Well I've got the buildings and good land for meadow hay, but buying in calves is a risky business especially when you've always been home-bred. Calves via markets can bring sick animals."

"I wasn't thinking of bought in calves Chas," Howard slipped into Charles' childhood nickname, "suppose you reared all the farm calves for Dad and me, and we upped the milkers to something over a hundred? You could still keep on with poultry and farm gate sales."

"But if you carry more milkers here, you'd need more acres if you were going in for Dad's idea of growing more cattle feed and buying less cake." This was from Jim.

"I think Howard has been exploring the idea of more land this last week or so." John winked at Howard across the room.

"Not half he hasn't," Ling burst in, "he's got his eye on Manor Farm, Brushstoke, it's for sale, but none of us really has the money. I've kept on telling him but he still keeps at it like a dog with a juicy bone."

"You're going on for a spanking, my little Wench." Howard hugged her as he spoke and grinned at everyone.

"Well I want to say something," said Mary, "I've been chatting to Kitty and the other two girls. We'd all love to have a farm-gate selling outlet, like a little shop. Kitty for her garden produce (Kitty had been selling fruit, flowers and vegetable from her big walled garden for some years) Gorse would like another outlet for her brown eggs and poultry. Ling and I would like a tearoom and perhaps do nice snacks for customers to the Farm Shop and/or Pick You Own fields." Everyone looked at Mary in amazement but she forged on bravely.

"Manor Farm would be ideal for that, it's eighty acres, main road position, nice buildings and everything in order including a lovely house. Is there any way we can try for it?"

"Now hold on folks," Charles' steady voice came in, "if, and it's a huge 'if', we could find the money, what about labour? A

Farm Shop needs someone to run it, pick your own fruit, well any sort of fruit is labour intensive, as Kitty will tell you, she's only grown strawberries since Nicky and Simon were older. Our twins take up a lot of Gorse's time and will do for a while yet. And then there's the tearoom. How many people are needed to run a tearoom?"

"Yes we don't want to put a damper on the ladies efforts, but we must think about labour." John spoke gently.

"May I say something?" Young Bill went bright red as spoke for the first time.

"Surely Lad, out with it."

"Well Daisy, my Daisy that is, she'd like real much to help, she's real keen on teashops and, well any sort of shop really. She wouldn't want a lot of money. She wants to stop near her Mam, helps with the younger ones she does. She'd just love to be asked to help." Very flustered now after so much talking, Bill lapsed into silence.

"And she'd be a most capable girl to help. I'm sure of that." Mary spoke up.

"Well from our end," Kitty spoke thoughtfully, "I've got a girl from the next village of ours, she comes and helps me. She would give some time over here and so would I. Now that Nicky and Simon are older I could easily spare time in the week and help in the shop, I would jump at the chance. And Jim's always game to help at weekends, on the farm side as you know."

"What about you Peter, would you come on the farm full time if we go into this mad venture?" Howard was smiling broadly now, as if something had pleased him greatly. He turned to look at Peter.

"Yes I would, I would. Since you ask, sounds like a good scheme, but oughtn't we to get back to the money?"

"Very difficult to do any sort of costing on labour requirements in a plan like this." John's firm voice came in.

"No, I agree. I think you would have to build it up slowly, bringing in labour and changes a little bit at a time. One thing .... I'd be glad to keep the books for you, I already do it for the

Church Council. Actually I rather enjoy doing it." Jim spoke in his usual quiet way.

"Well on the practical side, it would be the cooking part of the tearoom that I would be interested in. I could make scones, sponges, cakes and shortbread, lots of things like that. But I'd do it from here, where I could continue to be back-up for the two men and Bill when he's here. We might need another man later on, he could lodge here and take his meals with us, if we could get a nice Lad. The younger ones would have to run and organise the tearoom and shop. I'd love the cooking part. But I think we'll be stumped to buy Manor Farm in the first place, that's our biggest hurdle, the money. It's no use our worrying too much over who will do the work, to me that's easy, we're all used to hard work. A lot of girls round here would love a bit of part-time local work. There's plenty of young married women, nice country lasses in need of a few extra pounds in their purses. I expect there are in Brushstoke as well, right on site so to say." Mary stopped to get her breath after this enthusiastic offering.

"Just think, we could do cream teas, with our own Jersey Cream, and Mum's scones and make our own strawberry jam from the Pick Your Own strawberry field." Ling looked so excited that Howard leaned over and kissed her.

"You seem dead keen on the strawberries Lovelet, how many acres would you want?" Howard's voice was teasing.

"Well with Kitty so good at fruit, she would help us wouldn't you Kit? It would bring people out to the farm, then they'd want a cup of tea and a sit down after getting back-ache picking strawberries in the hot sun." Ling refused to be squashed.

"What about when it rained?" Howard was teasing again. Gorse decided to have a go.

"I think Ling's right, you men tend to carp on about details. And if it rains people would tend to come in and have a cup of tea, when it was too wet to pick fruit." Gorse popped her pink tongue out at Howard, who responded with like for like.

"Well now it's my turn, I think it's time to sum up and check our assets," John had a pad and pen on his lap, "to me it seems we all would like to have a go and would all be able and willing to give some help. I feel that we should take a vote, and if we all want to have a try we should then discuss what channels we could then approach to raise the money. Although I should tell you that I'm against a mortgage on the grounds that if farming is going to get tougher as time goes by, we shouldn't saddle ourselves with a stone round our necks which could make it even harder for the children who follow." John paused, to the sound of several, Here Here's from round the room.

"Mary and I could put up a couple of thousand but that would be in-roading into our savings. I would also say here that I don't think Charles should put money in. He is on a more difficult wicket than we are, and has only recently come into farming. The same ought to go for Jim and Kitty, they are not farming, so any help they can give in a practical way would be welcome but money is different. Mary and I discussed it, and we both felt that it would be robbing Nicky and Simon." John looked round, "Anyone want to say anything before we vote?"

"Yes, yes I do Dad, Ling and I have talked this out, Ling has £1000, savings and we jointly have about £1200 more, £500 from you and Mum after we got married and £700 we've saved up since. Mainly because we've had no rent or mortgage to pay, which again is down to you and Mum helping us so much." Howard stopped speaking and looked round the room. No one else spoke for a moment then Charles said quietly.

"We could do several hundred actually and would like to do so …. and the more I think about it the more interested I am in the whole scheme. Especially with Gorse and I as calf rearers," he paused and Jim chipped in,

"I've got a thousand doing nothing, I could put that in to fix a shop for Kitty's and everybody's produce, or to help buy the farm, whichever."

"Well I think it is a great credit to us all that we all want to help, and to help put up the money. Now shall we vote, show of hands or paper slips?" John asked.

"Show of hands." It came as a chorus.

"Right, who wants to have a go at buying Manor Farm so long as we don't have too big a mortgage? Hands up those for it." John raised his own hand as he spoke. Everyone's hand shot up including Peter's and Bill's

"Right that's settled then, how about some cocoa you girls and we'll set Howard, who started all this in the first place, to find out how much the farm is and if we've any hope. You'll have to buck up Lad, don't let anyone else get it All the lot of us are now desperate to have it so on your head be it." John sat back and began to fill his pipe once more and Mary and Ling stood up to go and make the cocoa. Howard sat back.

"Well, I'm glad to hear that." He said quietly.

"Glad to hear what?" Mary turned in the doorway.

"That it's on my head Mum and that everyone is so much in agreement." Mary looked at him questioningly.

"You see, as it happens, I bought Manor Farm a few days ago so it's quite fortunate you all want it."

"Howard," Ling's voice rose to a shriek as she hurled herself back across the room at him.

Bedlam broke loose, questions and answers crossed and re-crossed the room. No one could hear Howard's replies. Cocoa was forgotten. Mary sat down weakly in a chair. At last Ling made herself heard above the din.

"What about the money? You didn't even know if any of us could do any money." Indignation blazed out of Ling's eyes.

"Calm down Lovelet. I had the money, well almost and I knew that you would lend me a bit."

"You HAD the money? Where? .....," words failed her for a moment, "where did you get the money?" Her voice came now in a little squeak.

"Actually Howard Letts .... Uncle Howard Letts died in Canada and left me 16,000 Canadian Dollars, which in English money is £10,500."

A gasp went round the room, Mary was first to get her breath back.

"What that dreadful man, he was a ne'er-do-well, he left my

sister and her two girls years ago. I simply can't believe it."

"Actually Mum, he may have been all you say, but in the end he did very well. Again, he may have left them, but now he has left them well provided for. This money was what Dick Warren calls a small bequest for his namesake." Howard was enjoying himself enormously, watching everyones shocked and incredulous expressions.

"Howard." Ling had recovered her voice. "You devil you! All the time you knew! You knew! When I was worried about you being disappointed because we wouldn't be able to raise the money .... you knew .... it was in the letter, in the type-written letter from Canada, and you went to Banworth to find out from Dick Warren if it was true. So even when we went to see the farm you knew it was ours. You bought me a washing machine to keep my mind off the letter, you read that letter when I was asleep then you hid it. And ever since that night you've been sitting on 10,500 smackers while we all floundered about." Ling was red in the face with disbelief.

"I didn't want to hurt you if it wasn't genuine." Howard replied mildly. "How about a cup of cocoa Ma. Don't forget that Ma did just the same when she bought us Bunny Warren for a surprise .... before we got engaged. And she sighed a great sigh of relief when we really did get engaged soon afterwards. Like Mother Like Son. I was only following aged parents example." Howard was still grinning.

"Not so much of your aged parents talk Lad, and your Mother was not spending the kind of money you've just forked out." John waded in on Mary's behalf.

"Actually it's been painless Dad, I haven't paid a penny to anyone yet, that won't be for a week or two. But when Ling calms down I bet she'd rather have Manor Farm and all the fun it will bring to us all, than the actual money sitting in the bank. Anyway, as Granny would have said long ago, "'What's done is done' and you know how she liked buying property."

"I'll make the cocoa." said Mary faintly, rising from her chair and heading for the kitchen. Kitty, Ling and Gorse went to help her. Ling shot an .... 'I'll deal with you later' .... look at Howard as she passed his chair, but there was a twinkle in her eyes. The men, headed by John, agreed to meet again to discuss how best to arrange matters between them as fairly as possible, and how to form some sort of joint partnership of all their resources to help along their new venture.

After cocoa, the family split up and set off for home. The three elder children were woken to don coats over their pyjamas. The little ones were wrapped in rugs and mostly ferried to the cars while John took Mary's arm and guided her towards the stairs.

"No washing-up tonight Lass .... our Ling's coming early in the morning to give us a hand." Soon they were under the blankets.

"Just fancy our Howard, being left a fortune like that, and never saying a word. I can still hardly believe it .... and from that man, I just wonder how he made his money. Never had two half-pennies to rub together when we knew him." Mary's sleepy voice droned on.

"Well Lass let's just be thankful that Howard's had this windfall, just at the right moment, although I myself think it is more a gift from God than any sort of windfall. Anyway Lass, I think he's spent his money very wisely to secure a future for all the children. There now Love, we shall back him up all we can. Now let's get off to sleep."

STRAWBERRIES AND CREAM

Chapter 5

An Angel

STRAWBERRIES AND CREAM

Chapter 5

An Angel

Peter Radford whistled happily as he fed round the calves a few days later. He felt that his life had sorted itself out after a long period of unease. He was going to stay on, he had been uncertain before; his was a happy-go-lucky temperament and until a year or two back he had always been very easy-come, easy-go. Then he had had an unhappy love affair with a girl a bit older than himself. He had had girls before and had not cared deeply, but Elaine had been different. He had been very fond of Elaine and had been hurt when she threw him over for a man with clean hands and more money. That same week the garage had folded and he had lost his job.

When Peter arrived at Hill Farm, he had been in every way insecure, bruised and a trifle bitter. After the first week he had settled in, the warmth of his welcome and his easy friendship with Howard had enfolded him in easy goodwill and peace. He had enjoyed the farm life so much that he had then become worried lest he outstay his welcome with his Uncle and Aunt. Now everyone had come out in the open. They wanted him to stay, because of his cheerful presence in the house and they needed his help to build up the workforce for the extra land and the new project. All this contributed to his feeling of happiness and hope for the future. There was another small item. Yesterday Kitty Radford had come over with the girl who helped her with their market garden at their big country house some miles away. The girl's name was Angela, Angela Downing, but Kitty had introduced her as Angel,

"Everybody calls her Angel," said Kitty with a grin. Peter had kept in the background, but there was no doubt about it

Angel was a stunner. She was quite tall and she had red hair, a real bright cascade of red hair. That coupled with greenish eyes and a turned up freckled little nose and a mouth .... well Peter had been trying ever since to keep that mouth out of his mind, for he had no intention of complicating his happy new life at Hill Farm with falling for any more girls. While she was there Peter drank his mid-afternoon cup of tea and quickly excused himself, striding off across the yard to begin the round of yard work before milking.

Mary and John had welcomed the girl in their usual friendly way. She was, Kitty told them very good with soft fruit and was willing to come and help them to set up a small Pick Your Own area at Manor Farm. Howard talked to her at length, picking her brains about the varieties of strawberries and raspberries they might grow. The two of them stayed just over an hour, then Kitty drove them home having agreed that they all meet at Manor Farm the following week to look at the apple orchard and choose a good Pick Your Own site. Angel was keen that they get it ploughed down to a fine tilth in time to plant say a thousand strawberry plants in March while there was still rain about to set up the plants in the hope of getting a small crop this year and a really good one next year. Angel felt that it was too late to plant raspberries and that these would best be left until the following November.

Peter would have been surprised if he had heard Angel in the car as Kitty drove her home.

"Who was that quiet type with the fair curls and blue eyes and the sexy smile, who strode out across the yard before we had time to speak to him?" She asked Kitty.

"Oh that's Peter Radford, he's Mum and Dad Radford's nephew. He was working in a Coventry garage, it closed down so he came to help Howard overhaul the farm machinery. I think he was only going to stay for the month of February, but now they've bought this other farm he is going to stay on to swell the workforce for the extra eighty acres. He's nice, we all like him and he's a first-class mechanic. He lives in with Mum and Dad, I think both his parents are dead."

"I see, so I may meet up with him again?"

"Oh yes, he's part of Hill Farm staff now I'd say. He has always come to Hill Farm for holidays. Even as a child. He and Howard are great friends. I think he was coming long before Jim and I got married."

"Has he got a girlfriend?" Angels eyes twinkled as she asked the question.

"I think Mum said there had been a girl, but she chucked him for a man with more money. Surely you're not interested in him?"

"Not really, I just wondered about him, he seemed so determined to clear off the moment we arrived."

"I've never thought of Peter as shy or retiring, who knows perhaps your red hair bowled him over." Kitty swung the car into their own driveway as she spoke and pulled up at the garage doors.

"If you could close up the greenhouses for me Angel and then call it a day for today, I shan't try doing any more, it get's dark so early. You get off home. I'll be in the house getting a meal for Jim and the boys."

"I'll shut the greenhouses then, would you like me to shut the hen-pen doors as well, they'll all be gone in by then I should think."

"Oh Angel would you? That would save me putting on my wellies again."

"That's OK, see you in the morning." Angel vanished out of sight through the garden door.

The Radford men worked out a rough plan for the new project. Manor Farm was already in fact paid for. The legacy plus Ling and Howard's savings would see to that. It was to be their farm. They would move there. Providing Ling agreed.

67

Howard knew how she loved Bunny Warren, but it was also agreed that Bunny Warren cottage belonged with Hill Farm and should remain with it. Howard and Ling, with help from Kitty and Jim, both financial and practical, would get planning consent to convert the old stable at Manor Farm into a farm shop as soon as possible. Jim was to fill in the application forms at once. Kitty was to have a big share in the setting up, supplying and running of the shop.

The land from both farms would be used to support a larger dairy herd at Hill Farm. They would produce as much home-grown feed for the dairy cows as possible. Charles would continue to milk for the time-being, but would begin to convert some of the empty buildings at River Farm into a big calf unit. Later on they would transfer all the calf rearing to Charles and Gorse and then Charles would receive so much for each calf reared to come back into the dairy herd, and market the bull calves at Hampton-in-Arden Market. Then he could gradually move out of milking cows at River Farm.

The small fields near the house at Manor Farm would be used for fruit growing, which Ling would run with help from the farm side and from Angel and Kitty. Manor Farm would have one room converted to a tearoom. Gorse and Mary would both cook for both shop and tearoom from their own kitchens, being paid weekly for the goodies. Ling would run the tearoom with village help and Billy's Daisy full time when the tearoom was open. If Ling found time and wanted to she could do some Bed and Breakfast in the Summer. Gorse and Mary would be able to sell eggs and any other produce in the shop.

The milking at Hill Farm would still be shared by Howard, John, Bill and Peter, as would all the cultivation on both farms. It was only a rough plan but it was impossible so early on to see how everything would work out labour-wise. On the contract side they would continue to do work for other farmers if the workload did not become too heavy. It was also agreed that some money would be set aside each year in the hope that later it could be used to enlarge Charles' acreage if any land nearby came up for sale. When these details had been thrashed out they all turned their attention to field work, and getting things underway at Manor Farm.

Howard was soon up to his neck in lambing the flock of ewes, which he hoped another year to lamb at Manor Farm. For this year they went ahead as planned in a lambing area built a month before at Hill Farm. Howard's time being taken up with lambing, it left John and Peter to finish the preparation of all the machinery for the coming season. Everything was set aside however on the day that Kitty and Angel Downing came to help choose the strawberry and raspberry area at Manor Farm. They came in good time in the morning, because Kitty and Ling wanted to spend some time looking at the stables and talking over converting it into a shop. Jim had a friend who had agreed to draw a plan for them. After they had finished looking round and Kitty had made measurements to pass on to the man doing the drawings, they were invited to dinner at Hill Farm. At Hill Farm, delicious smells of roast beef were wafting from the Aga oven. The table was laid and Kitty, Ling and Angel were soon joined by Howard, Peter and John who came clumping across the yard, hungry for their dinners. Soon the whole party were sitting round the table and Ling was helping Mary dish up and serve. Peter found that Mary had seated Angel Downing almost opposite to him at the table. He found himself talking to Howard beside him but at the same time watching Angel under his eyelashes. She was very quiet, the chair beside her still empty until Mary was free to sit down after serving everyone. Peter's plate arrived in front of him, delicious slices of beef in gravy with a big spoonful of roast potatoes on the side. Dishes of carrots, peas and creamed potatoes, and a dish piled high with light-as-feathers yorkshire pudding, were set out for everyone to help themselves. Everyone settled down to enjoy the meal, and as the plates emptied chatter began to spread round the table.

"Any new lambs?" Mary looked across at Howard.

"Yes two more ewes this morning, and they've got two lambs each, and all four are ewe lambs, we're going well but the night-shift gets tiring." Howard smiled as he spoke, but Ling across the table thought how weary he looked. Lambing was always a tiring time for Howard. Angel looked across at Howard.

"I would love to see the baby lambs, would there be time before we go over to Manor Farm?" The greeny eyes sparkled and the tip-tilted nose and wide mouth underneath seemed to spill over with laughter. Peter drew in his breath and tried to concentrate on his plate.

"Surely, they're only just across the yard here, we'll go after dinner."

Angel turned to speak to Mary, and the red hair curled and swung about her shoulders. Peter put his knife and fork down thankful to have cleared his plate. Talk turned to the coming afternoon.

"I shall come with you this afternoon," Howard spoke between mouthfuls, "none of the ewes look like lambing and I'd like to be in on the choice of fruit areas."

"Well if we take two cars Angel and I can make tracks for home when we finish and be back in the daylight." Kitty suggested.

"Yes I'll bring the farm car, you come with me and Linglet and Peter too if Dad can spare him. We'll take the measuring tape and you can help me measure up, and between us we can keep these women within bounds, just in case they try to turn the whole farm over to fruit."

"We shan't want much to start, but in that position, with the main road so handy, you'll soon want to add to the amount of fruit. When the money comes rolling in, you wait and see." Angel's eyes lit up as she spoke. Again Peter found his eyes on her and this time she felt his glance and turned her head to look at him full in the face for the first time. Peter felt himself drowning in that look. He couldn't draw his eyes away. She was so alive and so sure of herself. For Angel it was just as devastating, she could not face his look. She dropped her eyes feeling the colour rush up her neck and face. Mary, who was not born yesterday, slipped easily into the tense silence.

"I'm sure John will spare Peter, but I would love to come too if there's a space in the car. I've not been round the house, I'm longing to see it." Ling, who had noticed nothing, was delighted with this idea.

"Oh yes Mum, lovely idea. Peter and Howard will be ages measuring up, we can have a womens natter about the tearoom." Mary and Ling were by now clearing the plates and serving the steamed lemon pudding. Mary sliced the pudding and Ling went round the table pouring on hot lemon sauce. Mary produced a jug of thick Jersey cream which she passed round after the sauce.

"My favourite pudding Mother, even the smell of it gets to me before I even take a mouthful. How shall I be able to bend in the field this afternoon?" Kitty lifted her spoon savouring the lemon flavour pudding before putting it in her mouth.

"Everything Mum cooks is scrummy." said Howard who had more than an eye on Peter, who he was sure had been hit by a thunderbolt by all that red hair opposite. Do him a power of good the old stodge-pot, was Howard's reaction. Just what Peter needs, a luscious armful like that. Time he got settled in life like the rest of us. With these amused private thoughts Howard began to tuck into his pudding.

After dinner the women cleared the table and tidied up. Howard took Angel across to see the lambs. The washing up was taken over by John, insisting that they could all get off more quickly if he took over washing the rest of the dishes. He was the only one left standing on the yard to wave the cars off. Young Bill having gone across to check on the ewes in the far lambing pen, just to be on the safe side.

When the cars reached Manor Farm, the whole party went first to look at the two pasture fields. Mary was very taken with the grassy tree-topped mound in the larger field, but it was to the other field that Angel led them. Clad now in short wellies over her trim slacks, she stood for some minutes looking carefully about her before walking across the field with the mound in it and on into the other small field, which had as a Southern

71

boundary, the Manor House garden wall. Then there was a gentle slope up towards the reservoir bank. Angel walked across the turf, back again and then up to the top hedge by the reservoir bank. At last she spoke.

"Let's have a look at the soil here Howard, this is a lovely slope, due South, lovely for strawberries if it's free draining."

Howard was carrying a spade. He drove it into the turf and turned a spadeful of sandy loam. A smile lit Angel's eyes and Peter felt his heart leap.

"I'd call that nearly perfect, not too light not too heavy." She turned her smile on Peter but did not actually meet his eyes.

"Now Peter, it is PETER isn't it?" Almost she winked at him. "Yes Peter, could you measure from the fence here down to the garden wall, by the oak tree down there and then across the field to the other hedge, to get the area? This piece of land would suit our purpose. It would accommodate a thousand plants. Cambridge 422 is the one I would recommend. That is the Cambridge Favourite, it is an old variety but it is a good doer and very drought resistant. The fruit has a good shape and colour and a lovely flavour. Also the leaf is nice, it looks fresh and green and the strawberries bunch nicely on the plants. Also I can get a thousand plants easily for three weeks today."

"Three weeks? We'll never be ready in three weeks will we?" This from Howard.

"Yes easily, it's only a small area. After it's ploughed, disced and harrowed, I suggest you buy a Mayfield Garden Tractor with all its tools, then you can easily work this amount of ground and the weeds won't get on top of whoever is responsible for keeping it weed-free."

"Is it a man's work? How big is a Mayfield?" This question came from Ling who had been listening to every word.

"Oh no I often use one, I'll give you a couple of addresses where they supply Mayfields. You'd handle it easily enough. Ling or Kitty or anyone used to gardening."

"Where do we get the strawberry plants?" asked Howard.

"Well I'll contact Ted Moult, he supplies lovely plants.

"D'you mean the farmer come broadcaster?" asked Mary. "He's on that quiz show on TV."

"Yes that's the man, he will be very fair with you." Angel's eyes were following Peter who helped by Kitty was measuring across the bottom of the area she had chosen.

"What will the plants cost?" asked Howard.

"£4 a thousand."

"Golly, that doesn't seem much."

"It isn't much, why don't you double the site and have two thousand? You won't regret it I promise." The red hair danced about her head and a laugh burst from her lips. Howard could understand why Peter had been knocked out by this lovely girl. Perhaps she would be beyond his reach. Even as the thought came Howard saw her eyes again seek out and follow Peter across the field. Well perhaps she was smitten too. They all stood and watched until Peter and Kitty were back with them with the area measured and the measurements written down in Howard's notebook. Soon they were walking back to the gate.

"Shall we do two thousand Howard? It's not a big area." Asked Ling.

"The Mayfield and all its tools, scuffles, hoes and grass cutter, which you will need to keep green pathways short cut for easy walks for pickers, will cost you £150/200, but it means easy care of the site. To keep it really nice and inviting to customers. So it's well worth the money laid out." Angel explained.

"I think we should have the two thousand, as Angel feels so sure they will do well. What about raspberries?" Howard spoke with more enthusiasm than he had yet shown.

"You wouldn't grow really good raspberries here. It will be too warm and dry during Summer. I think for raspberries, just beyond the buildings, where the apple trees are. I saw them from the road. It's more shady there. If the soil is a bit heavier there then so much the better, that's what raspberries need. We could plant in November, but no real crop for two years. But after that; quite an expensive fruit to buy even with Pick Your Own. Malling Promise is a good reliable variety. Let's go and look. The party went across to the buildings and through the passage to the orchard area. Mary and Ling left them and went into the house. Mary was enchanted with it all especially the great big kitchen and the lovely sitting room just along a short length of passage. Mary visualised this as a tearoom fed by the big cool kitchen. Ling wasn't quite so sure. She wondered if the huge kitchen could become the actual tearoom, looking as it did straight across to the stable, which would soon be the farm shop. The two large pantries beyond would then become kitchens. They discussed it in friendly fashion.

"Anyway Love it's a dear old house, shall you and Howard be happy here? Or will you miss the cottage? You've been so happy there I know that." Mary asked a trifle anxiously.

"Wherever Howard is I shall be happy, I do love the cottage. I shall always treasure our time there. But this place is for Sally Anne and Richard, and for all the family mum, we'll be fine here, come and see the garden, the jasmines out on the wall." Ling smiled very sweetly at Mary, no-one should ever know her hurt at leaving Bunny Warren, and anyway she told herself sternly this was a lovely farm and was going to be a home with a capital 'H' for Howard. Mary watched the lovely expression on her daughter-in-law's face and for the hundredth time thanked God for her son's choice of a wife. Their happiness was very much the gilt on her ginger-bread.

Anyway Bunny Warren is still in the family. Perhaps some other member of the family may live there next." Ling wanted Mary not to worry.

"Like Peter perhaps?" Mary smiled a naughty little smile.

"Oh and the red-head you mean? What a bombshell she is. D'you think I should be watching Howard Mum?"

"You'll never need to watch Howard, he loves you so much; more than he did when he married you if that's possible." Mary smiled fondly.

"She knows her job, as Kitty said, she knows all about fruit. I wonder if she'll help us plant the strawberries, I'd like to see her get her hands dirty."

"I think if Peter helps plant the strawberries then she might easily too." Mary smiled as she spoke.

"Kitty says she works like a black in their garden and greenhouses, and Kitty would certainly not employ her unless she was a good worker. She is a very pretty girl, lovely smile, bet she's got a temper on her when the mood takes her." Mary was enjoying mulling Angel over in her mind.

"Oh Mum you are a card, you're marrying her off to Peter in your mind already."

"Well you've got to admit, I've not done badly so far. Three smashing daughters-in-law and all these beautiful little grandchildren. Only problem, only one pattern, these Radford men."

"Now you can't say that about my Howard. Sally Anne is a real little girl." was Ling's response.

"Have you thought Lass?" Mary walked carefully down the Manor staircase as she spoke. "Have you thought that we might be in luck?"

"I should have thought that we were definitely in luck. Look at Howard's windfall."

"I know Lass, a real miracle that was, but that's not what I'm on about." They went out of the back door just as the others came back through the buildings.

"What I meant was perhaps Peter and his red-head might have the other pattern. I quite fancy a few little red-headed girls in the family."

"Oh Mum, you're a lovely Mum but you may be barking up the wrong tree this time." Ling took Mary's arm and they walked across the yard to join the others.

———————

A week later Mary was in her garden weeding. Peter had cut the grass for her and the first daffodils were bursting bud. Along the wall of the house the forsythia was full of yellow flowers, and in the soil in the narrow border beneath, the polyanthus were coming out in shades of yellow and red and orange. Mary loved her garden, much of the weeding she did sitting on a stool, now that her joints were stiff. The vegetable area Howard helped with, digging it over for her every Autumn. Peter had planted three rows of early potatoes for her that morning and promised to sow peas and carrots later on. From the garden she could see the ewes with their lambs at play in the front fields. Down on the reservoir the pair of swans were busy building their nest on a strip of land which jutted out into the water. There were also moorhens and wild duck busy about their Spring duties. Along the lane in Aunty Nell's field she could see the Jersey cows cropping the short Spring grass. They were out in the daytime now, and young Bill was having a Spring-clean of the cow cubicles with tractor and fork-loader. Mary could hear him shunting about with the machinery.

John was in the house writing up the farm books which had to go to the accountant by the end of March. Mary stood up to rest her back. Going down the path she leant on the front gate. Across the reservoir she could see Howard on the tractor ploughing the runs for the strawberries. When he came up the slope of the field, she could see him and the tractor until he turned to go back down again.

Across the water, Howard, Peter, Kitty and Angel were all involved in preparing the site. It needed careful ploughing. They wanted to plough out eight narrow, one yard wide strips, leaving the other turf intact so as to make grassy walks for strawberry pickers to be able to get to the plants. Peter, Kitty and Angel were busy with spades, tidying back any places where the plough had run over the grass. All were in working clothes. Howard was almost done, he shouted to Peter above the din of the engine.

"Can you start the other tractor and disc behind me Pete? I'll be done shortly."

"Right, I'll fetch the other set of tackle." Peter shoved his spade in the ground, smiled at the two girls and strode off towards the farmyard.

76

"What a lovely dishy man." Angel grinned at Kitty.

"Yes and I think he quite likes you too." Kitty stretched her shoulders back.

"Well he's very slow saying so."

"Radford men are slow but sure, maybe he'll surprise you soon. Here he comes now." Peter drove into the field. He was on the smallest tractor they had. A little Ford-Dexta. Behind it was a narrow small set of discs which John and Peter had constructed themselves in the farm workshop. Soon Peter was toiling up and down the ploughed runs, the circular cutting discs slicing down the ploughed furrows to a much finer tilth. Not as experienced as Howard, it took Peter all his time to keep the machine in a straight line. Howard had finished, he came across and picked up Peter's spade and went across to the first ploughed strip, to tidy in the edges once more, this time after the discs had been through.

An hour later Peter had finished, parking his tackle by the garden wall, and came to the others who were about half done. Howard looked up and spoke.

"That's fine, it's going to come good, needs harrowing next, have to use just one harrow and do it twice I expect. Think we shall need to roll it Kitty?"

"Let's see how dry it comes after harrowing, no use getting it too solid before we plant." Kitty pushed back her hair as she spoke. Angel bent and picked up a sample of soil in her grubby hand. Peter watched her every move with interest, but she pretended not to notice him.

"I'll take the plough tackle back and get to the ewes again. I've at least two I think will lamb today. Mum says all come up for dinner. There's flasks and mugs here with a drink, I forgot. You have them, Mum'll have the kettle on when she hears me coming up." Howard reached the old leather bag from off the tractor and handed it to Kitty.

"See you at dinner time." He grinned and set off across the fields heading for the tunnel under the railway which would take him back into Hill Farm fields. Kitty set aside her spade,

"I'll have to go across to the house toilet before I can enjoy a drink. No doubt you can manage for five minutes." Her last remark was lost on the other two. Peter reached for the flasks watching Kitty's retreating back. He carefully poured out two mugs of coffee. Handing one to Angel, he caught her sleeve and drew her towards the garden wall. At his touch her eyes flew up to meet his and to find him laughing at her discomposure.

"Here sit down, we deserve a rest, sit on this sack it's dry." He moved across to the tractor seat and took the sack which was folded as a cushion and set it on the wall for her. She sat down and with eyes lowered began to sip her drink.

"The field is going to come really good, where did you learn so much about strawberries Miss Strawberry Curls?" He kept his voice very ordinary so as not to increase her nervousness.

"Oh I had three years at Harper Adams, studying horticulture and I became especially interested in soft fruit."

"You don't look that old. You must have been doing that while I was learning the insides of cars from my Dad. Did your Mother have glorious hair like yours or are you a one-off?"

"I suppose I'm a one-off, Mums hair is dark. And some people don't like my red hair I may tell you." A little smile broke as she spoke, tipping the wide mouth to show very even white teeth.

"Well," Peter decided to jump in the deep end, "well," he continued calmly, "it was certainly that wonderful mane of hair and your ridiculous little nose that made me fall head-over-heels in love with you the first moment that I laid eyes on you."

He heard her draw in her breath, but did not look up at her. Instead he continued drinking his coffee and looking up towards the house. He saw Kitty coming across the grass.

"Ah, there you are, let me pour a mug of coffee, we've been resting on our laurels for five minutes, but we shall have to get on or we shall be late for Mary's dinner."

"I've just locked up the house again Peter, you take the key for Howard, he doesn't really get possession for another three weeks. We've been given permission to work the land I gather until then." Kitty handed the big key to him. Peter put it in the tractor tool box.

"This tractor is to stay here, in the tractor house. So if we all know where the key is, we can find it if we need the toilet."

Soon they were at work again. On the now finer tilth it was easier to get tidy at the edges and by just after twelve noon they were finished.

"We'll go home in my car, it's in the yard." Kitty wiped her spade off with a handful of grass as she spoke. Peter took Angel's spade and cleaned it off against his own.

"We'll lock them up in the shed, I've got the key, at least I know where it's hidden." Soon they were in the car speeding towards the farm. Peter had held the door of the front seat open for Angel and then climbed in the back. He sat behind Angel and couldn't resist her hair which overhung the seat in front of him. He reached out and fingered a curl, twirling it round and round on his finger until it tightened against her head.

"Leave my hair alone, what on earth do you think you're doing," she almost snapped at him, as she jerked her head away.

"Oh I'm wooing you my Angel, hadn't you realised?" Peter had laughter in his voice.

"But you can't. I've only known you a couple of weeks, and anyway in front of Kitty, it's so embarrassing." Angel's cheeks were almost the same colour as her hair.

"All right I'll stop wooing you but not for long. Here's Hill Farm and it's dinner time. I'm famished, I can just do with one of Aunt Mary's dinners."

The rest of the day had a very unreal quality for Angel. Peter never lost a chance to be near her and paid her every possible attention. She was determined to keep him at a distance. She felt very flustered, that she hardly knew him, and that everything was happening too fast and too soon. She also felt so much attraction towards him that she was as afraid of herself as of him. It was with relief that she saw the end of the day's work.

The ground for the strawberries was harrowed and neat. A fine tilth ready for planting. They were all tired out and Kitty was glad to climb into the car and head for home and a hot bath. Angel sank into the passenger seat and closed her eyes as they drove out of Manor Farm gates.

"You look exhausted, or is it just Peter getting you down?" Kitty sounded so sympathetic that it almost reduced Angel to tears.

"It was a tiring day, and I'm so unsure, I mean he's very attractive, but I don't want to be made a fool of in front of everybody. Do you think he's serious? I don't see how he can be. We don't know each other, it's only two weeks."

"Does the amount of time make any difference? Are you serious about him? That's what you've got to think about." Kitty drove along the tree-lined road towards home.

"I think it's because I like him so much that I'm afraid that he may let me down if I let him see that I care."

"Radford men are not usually fickle, they see what they want and go for it. I think Peter's fallen for you hook, line and sinker, so does Howard." Kitty thought she was being reassuring, but Angel was too tired.

"Everybody seems to know it all except me. I'm going to avoid Peter for a while."

STRAWBERRIES AND CREAM

Chapter 6

Planting Strawberries

STRAWBERRIES AND CREAM

Chapter 6

Planting Strawberries

And so it was, that when the strawberry plants arrived by rail a few days later. Angel stayed at home to work in Kitty's greenhouses, pricking out boxes of bedding plants, and the strawberry planting gang consisted of Howard and Ling, who left the children with Mary; and Peter and Kitty. It was a lovely day, the first really Spring-like day they had had. Putting the bushy plants in was easy work. Each person had a trowel and a pack of plants. Each took a length of prepared ground and set the first three plants across the top end of the ground. This was repeated every eighteen inches until the whole length of prepared ground was filled up. Each plant was firmed with the heel of the planter.

It took them the full day to plant the 2000 plants. It was a wearying day for Peter. He had thought to spend the day working alongside Angel and found it a hard task to hide his disappointment. Why hadn't she come? He worried about it all day. When the planting was finished, Kitty, who had worked alongside a rather glum Peter all day, decided to come to his rescue.

"I think you frightened Angel off Peter, she was all set to come but cried off at the last minute. She doesn't know you very well and I think that she is not half as brazen as her hair might suggest. I think my advice would be to slow down a little bit. Let her see how much you care, but slowly, don't rush her. Also why not keep it private between the two of you? Sort of softly, softly catchy monkey." Kitty was smiling as she spoke.

"But suppose she doesn't come again?" Peter looked quite downcast at the thought.

"I'm sure she will, Howard's going to need help with

preparing the raspberry ground when the lambing's finished. Angel is coming to help. It can't be planted up until November but the two acres are to be ploughed and made ready. The posts and wire supports sited and put in. Sometime next week I think Howard said."

Peter had to accept this and try not to show his depression to the rest of the family. Mary, seeing his gloom a few days later, when he came into the kitchen when she was taking a batch of shortbreads out of the Aga oven, decided to wade in herself.

"Now then young Peter, John and I are lost without our cheery nephew. Sit you down in that chair and I'll make us a cup of tea. She suited the action to the words and was soon pouring a big mug of hot sweet tea.

"Now get that down you and get outside these," she broke off two large pieces of the still warm shortbread and pushed them into his hand. She patted his shoulder, sipped her own tea and continued setting her cooking to cool. A slow smile crossed Peter's face as he took a bite out of the tasty shortbread.

"You know exactly the way to a man's heart Aunt Mary. This tastes out of this world."

"Well don't tell Howard, as a rule I won't let him come picking tasty tit-bits when I'm busy cooking."

"I won't say a word. Now I must get back to work. Uncle John wants to sow the oats tomorrow."

"Well, there now, two things before you go. She thought YOU might just be sowing your wild oats, you've got to show her you're serious. the second thing is that true love never runs smooth, so console yourself with that my Lad."

"What should we all do without you Aunt Mary?"

"Don't know. You men, you're just a lot of big kids you are."

"OK point taken," and he was gone.

———————

At Hill Farm Spring was getting well under way. The March

winds dried the fields. The lambs grew daily on the sweet young grass. The milk from the cows grew creamier day by day as the pastures sweetened and the white clover came into growth. In the garden at Bunny Warren Ling enjoyed the scent of the wallflowers and primroses in the orchard bank. The robins began to build their usual nest near the oak tree in the moss above the stream. Ling wept a few secret tears over her garden. She loved it so. She did not deceive Howard, and one lunch-time when he came through the garden gate, he found her having a little cry amongst her flowers.

"Oh my love, my own precious, don't cry. I shouldn't be putting you through this, it's my fault. I went and bought Manor Farm without thinking. When you love it so much here." She was in his arms and he was wiping her eyes with his big hanky.

"Oh no, no Howard. I love the farm, really I do, it's only, only the scent of the wallflowers, and because, because this has always been our place. I'm so afraid the little rabbit will miss us, and perhaps no one will come, I know it is silly."

"Darling, darling .... of course it's not silly." He drew her across to the garden seat and cuddled her against him.

"Now sweetheart, we shall take the little stone rabbit with us, and this garden seat. they are part of the family now aren't they? And we shall take lots of snippets of all your special plants. Then your sweet little green fingers will make them grow in the new garden at Manor Farm. You will have the fun of the Pick Your Own, and the tearoom, and have me about much more in our own farmyard. And my poppet we will come back and tend this little garden and look after the cottage until Mum finds someone else to live here."

"Oh Howard, you always cheer me up. I will see more of you round the yard, and in and out for elevenses. I'd never thought of that."

"Feel better now then? How about some dinner?"

"It's all ready, I'll fetch the pram, it's in the orchard. Richard's in the orchard too, in his play-house." Howard watched with relief as she went to fetch Sally Anne's pram. It was two weeks to their move, and he knew some of it would not be easy for either of them.

At Hill Farm the oats had been sown and ten acres of barley. The weather had been with them and John and Howard had also sown fifty acres for other local farmers, which was keeping the contract business going better than they had dared to hope. They were now preparing the fields, thirty-eight acres in all, of ploughed land at Manor Farm. It was to be sown with oats, barley and mixed corn for cattle feed which they would grind and mix for themselves. After more than half this had been sown John decided that Howard should have a few days to help Ling get their new home ready. Peter, John felt, could do with the experience of drilling corn. Howard was glad, he felt it would ease the move for Ling. The curtains for the new house were made and ready to hang. Gorse, who was a wonderful girl with a sewing machine, had done all the making up. Ling had chosen a chintz material for all the main rooms. Mary had given her the lining material. For the kitchen and back rooms Howard had fancied a plain green leaf design cotton material which they had spotted in Banworth. Ling and Mary had cut out and tacked up the curtains and then Gorse had taken them all to River Farm and spent many hours making them up. Howard and Ling spent their first day getting all the curtains up. At once the house looked more homely. They had bought a second-hand four-oven Aga, and this had been installed in the kitchen, at the end where the old chimney had served an old-fashioned iron range. Installation had been done neatly and the cooker tiled round. Howard ordered coke and lit the Aga resolving to keep it going, to warm the house until they moved in.

"Isn't it lovely and warm in here now, getting more like home." Ling was getting enthusiastic about it all.

"I suggest we go over to that second-hand furniture warehouse in Leamington, and see what we can get in the way of furniture and carpets." Howard suggested.

"Can we afford to buy, Howard?"

"I totted up and I think we can manage £150/200, we need

carpets and some big pieces of furniture, old-fashioned I think don't you? We need to fill these big rooms and make it homely."

"Oh that would be lovely, just the two of us go and choose."

The next day found them in Leamington walking round the big two-storey warehouse for second-hand goods.

"We'll walk all round first and make some notes in my pad. Then we could go and have a snack in a milk-bar, work out the money and decide what we want most. Then come back and buy early this afternoon." Howard suggested.

They looked at carpets first and chose two big squares of Wilton for the two main bedrooms. It was a plain dark coffee shade. They cost £5 each which they felt was a good start. The rug in reds, blues, mustard and brown turkey style, which they chose for the front hall, to match the existing turkey stair carpet was more money and was £15. Howard was determined to have it as it was in such good condition and such a good match. They then found a greeny/browny Indian carpet for one sitting room and the other would be covered by the sitting room carpet from Bunny Warren. The Indian was in good condition and was also £15. Small rugs were pricey so they left them alone and went into the furniture section. Here they chose a three-piece suite for £12. It was large and roomy, covered in faded chintz which almost matched the new curtains. Two comfortable armchairs in faded brown linen covers, at £3 each were to go by the Aga in the kitchen. There were a lot of antiques and near antiques when it came to upright chairs, but they chose twelve Windsor style really strong chairs in stained pine to go round the big kitchen table. They were a real bargain at £1 each. Two nice ladder-backs for the hall, solid oak, hand rushed were six pounds each but again Howard felt that they were well worth the money.

Ling turned her attention to the bedrooms. Beds they found were cheap. The main bedroom furniture would come from the cottage. The other large bedroom in their new home was the room they had to buy for. They chose a pair of Regency style walnut beds with little insets of cane-work in the bed-heads. A low walnut dressing-table, and a big wardrobe which almost matched, cost a total of £14 which both felt was very reasonable. Three Lloyd-Loom armchairs in pink and gold were £1 each. Then they saw a child's bed with little brass bobbles on it. It at once caught Ling's eye.

"Oh Howard could we get that for Richard? I can just see it with a patchwork quilt on and his teddies sitting on the pillow."

"It's a nice little bed and it's only a couple of pounds. D'you think Sally Anne would like the rocking horse as well?"

"I hadn't seen that, how much?"

"Three pounds, let's get it, and let's try for something else for Richard, I'd like a little desk and nice chairs for his room."

They found a plain oak nineteen-thirties desk for a child, with drawers, and two chairs padded with soft arms. Also a small wardrobe with drawers down one side. These they bought for Richard's room at a total cost of £12.

"We've done so well, let's try and furnish the fifth bedroom with a double bed for visitors." Howard was getting really keen now. Then they found the best bargain of all. A bedroom suite with double oak bed, and a large old-fashioned dressing-table and with it a three-quarter oak wardrobe, with a long mirror down the front. The whole suite was £22.

"Let's speak for it all now Howard, and get lunch after, in case we lose anything. There's not many people here now but there may be more customers later." Ling looked pleadingly at Howard.

"Just my idea Linglet, let's sit on this settee of our suite and tot up what we've spent." Howard totted up his list with a stub of pencil.

"One hundred and thirty-eight pounds in all, well I'm blessed. Isn't that good? D'you want anything else Lass?"

"Could we make it up to £150 with some bedding at Lovats, just up the road?"

"Yes we could, we'll spend £25 on blankets and sheets and what-nots to give you a start. Let's arrange delivery, and pay for the furniture first. I'm hoping they can deliver tomorrow."

Howard was delighted that they had chosen so well and

managed to keep the cost down as well. They found the Manager who went with them and made a list to match Howards. While they went round Ling walked through again and found two oak stools for 10/- each and a pile of down cushions with no price on. On consulting the Manager, he smilingly took the £1 cash from her for the stools and said she could have the cushions free as they had bought so much. He also agreed to deliver next day, early afternoon. Howard and Ling carried stools and cushions to lock in the car boot, and went in search of a milk-bar. Over hot coffee and ham rolls they discussed their purchases.

"I'm longing to go to Manor Farm and polish the floors and be there to welcome the man with the load tomorrow. Oh Howard it's going to look so nice. Haven't we been lucky?"

"Yes it's almost another windfall isn't it Linglet? Let's eat up and go and get that bedding for all these new beds."

"Yes, yes let's." For £25 they got four pairs of plain sheets, twelve pillow cases and three folk-weave bedspreads in plain cream material, two single and one double. Ling also bought half a dozen plain green towels which were on a bargain.

They got home to Hill Farm in time for the mid-afternoon cup of tea. Both their children were as usual perfectly happy with Mary. Mary fetched out the fruit cake and Ling and Howard had a big slice each, sitting at the kitchen table while Mary and Ling went through Howard's list of purchases. Mary was thrilled with it.

"I shall want to come and look when you've got it all there and nicely placed. What a lot of bargains, it's a new home nearly isn't it Lass?"

It had been a lovely but tiring day and Howard and Ling were glad to get back to Bunny Warren and cook their supper. They went to bed early and slept like tops, only to be woken by Sally Anne at 7.00 next morning. Howard got up and made tea and took it up to Ling. They sat in bed with Sally Anne between them while they drank the tea and discussed the day's plans. They decided to take the children to see their future home and let them play and enjoy the house while they polished up the floors and waited for the furniture to come in. A picnic was obviously the answer. After breakfast Howard got the children ready while Ling cut sandwiches and packed cake and biscuits to take with them. She packed cups and saucers, tea, milk and sugar and an old kettle and teapot.

"We can make hot drinks on the Aga."

"Yes we can, put in some extra mugs, Dad and Pete may be drilling one of the fields. We can invite them in for a cuppa." Howard grinned and went to put the pushchair in the back of the car, which he had again borrowed from Hill Farm. Arrived at Manor Farm, they went first with the children to see how the strawberry plants were settling in. There had been a shower of rain overnight and the leaves on the plants were beginning to show new green as they became established.

"Our first crop here, they look really good don't they?"

"Yes they look great. I think that I can hear the tractor in the big corn field. Sounds as if Dad and Pete are drilling the mixed corn." Ling looked up and she too could hear the tractor across the fields.

"You go and see how they're getting on, take Richard with you. I'll take the pushchair back and open up the house. Richard's got his wellies on. D'you want to go with Daddy and see Grandad?" Ling smiled as Richard's eyes lit up.

"I can easily walk over there." Richard waved his arms towards the tractor's sound.

"Come on son, we'll tell Grandad to come for a cup of tea in our new house later on." Ling watched them across the field and then pushed Sally Anne towards the house. Before long she had got brooms and mop polishers out of the car and a rug to sit Sally Anne on with her toys. Picnic things she put on the kitchen table. Then she filled the kettle and put it on the Aga low plate. Howard would fuel the Aga when he came in. She started on the front sitting room floor, first spreading the rug for Sally Anne and her toys. The little girl was for pushing herself along the floor and exploring the area her Mother was busy polishing.

"It's a good thing you've got trews on my lady or you'd

surely get a splinter in your bottom." Sally Anne took this to be a great joke and gurgled at her Mum before continuing her crab-like progress across the floor. Ling fetched more toys from the bag in the kitchen, plonked them on the rug and heaved the little girl back to base. Sally Anne settled down to play with her toys.

"Now be a good girl and let Mummy get on with the work."

Howard joined her soon after and during the next hour and a half they moved from room to room, rubbing and polishing the old oak floors. Ling took a bucket which she fortunately found under the sink, as she'd never thought to bring one. With hot water from the kettle she wiped down the window sills and skirting boards as they moved from room to room, carrying Sally Anne's blanket along with them. John and Peter found them hard at work when they came across the fields in search of a cup of tea later in the morning.

"Anyone in? How about that cup of tea?" John's cheerful voice came from below.

"Here Dad, upstairs, we're clearing the decks for the furniture delivery." Howard shouted down the stairs.

"No, we'll come down, I've got the kettle on ready." Ling picked up Sally Anne off the front bedroom floor and thrust her into Howard's arms.

"Come on, you bring her and I'll get the tea on," she ran quickly down to the kitchen to greet the two men.

"How've you got on? Is the field sown yet?" Ling busied herself with mugs and tea making.

"We're well on Lass, over half done, finish by dinner time. It's a lovely soil, the seeds going in real smooth isn't it Peter?" Peter, rough in his working overalls, his hair tousled and a tumble of wild fair curls, was looking round the kitchen.

"Yes it's a nice easy ride field compared with the last ten acres at Hill Farm last week." Ling was pouring tea and she handed Peter a large mugfull. He carried it across to the window-seat and sat down. Howard coming into the room with Sally Anne in his arms, and little Richard hard on his heels, couldn't help thinking that Peter had turned into a real farmer these last few weeks. He looked fitter and broader. His skin had caught the Spring sunshine and the wind. If that red-head didn't look a bit sharp and snap him up some other girl damn soon would. Which would be a pity thought Howard as he handed Sally Anne to her Grandad and picked up his mug of tea.

"When're Kitty and Redilocks coming again? D'you know Peter?" Howard asked innocently.

"No I know nothing about it except that they're coming to help sort out the raspberry area site." Peter buried his nose in his tea mug.

"Kitty said give her a ring when the fields were seeded, should be finished tomorrow I reckon." John was bouncing the little girl on his knee in the window-seat.

"I'll give her a ring tonight, don't you think Howard? Then most likely she and Angel can fit in coming on Monday." John put the child down and began to drink his tea. Sally Anne set off across the kitchen floor on her bottom.

"This is a smashing kitchen, you could sit twenty people in here round this table." Peter was still taking in his surroundings.

"Yes I'm wondering if we ought to use this as the tearoom, instead of the sitting room. Make it a farmhouse kitchen tearoom. Check cloths, ham and eggs, that sort of thing. Use the back door as the entrance. People could come in straight out of the stable farm shop and leave their cars parked in the yard. We'd only have to give it up as a private kitchen during opening hours from Easter until September. When there would be people about in the countryside wanting teas." Ling looked across at Howard as she spoke.

"Even with the Aga at the far end, I suppose people might like to watch, and smell their ham and eggs being cooked, it would certainly be less far to carry tea trays." Howard suggested with a grin.

"I never thought of that, we'll have to talk it out, but for the moment I must get done with the rooms, so we can have our picnic before the furniture comes." Ling began to collect up the mugs.

"Back to the grindstone then Pete." John got up and Peter followed him outside. Howard and Ling finished the floors and then sat on the kitchen window-seat with Richard and Sally Anne to eat their picnic. Almost as soon as they had finished the van arrived with the furniture. The driver chose to park inside the yard and carry in through the big back doorway. All the doorways were wide and roomy, and it meant that their vehicle was off the main road. Everything was quickly unloaded, and with Howard and Ling to direct the placing of each item, things rarely needed to be handled twice. Ling felt afterwards that the moment all the things they had chosen were in place, just a little shabby and worn as it was; the house at once turned into a home. Howard saw it in her face, when they walked through all the rooms after the men had gone.

"It'll be even better when our own things come from Bunny Warren," he said putting his arm about her shoulders.

"Yes it's getting really homely. The only thing I do think is that we ought to have had twenty four of those Windsor chairs. They had a lot more of them and they would be ideal for the tearoom, wherever we decide to have it."

"I'll give them a ring when we get home, I think we should make tracks Love, the kids are tired with so much hub-bub and I am on early turn for milking in the morning. It's back to work tomorrow don't forget."

"I'm not tired, I like this big house and the fields and Peter and Grandad coming. Can I see which is to be my very own room before we go home Dad?" Richard had come running in from the farmyard.

"You show him Howard, while I mind Sally Anne and pack up the picnic things." Ling began to collect everything from the kitchen. She left the kettle and teapot, and the mugs turned on the draining board for next time.

A few minutes later they were heading for Hill Farm to take John's car back. Howard had decided privately that he was going to buy a small vehicle of their own before the move, and teach Ling to drive so that she would be able to take Richard to school when he started after the Summer holidays. She would also be able to get to the shops off her own bat when they moved to Manor Farm.

When they got back to Bunny Warren Howard phoned to secure another dozen of the Windsor kitchen chairs, which the Manager promised would be delivered in a few days C.O.D. Howard then rang Kitty about Monday re the raspberry site. Kitty was free to come on the Monday and said she would bring Angel with her. The next few days passed quietly, Howard was back at work. The men were finishing drilling corn at Manor Farm. Lambing was almost over. There had been only three lambs born during Howards time off. At the cottage, Ling began to pack china and small items into cardboard boxes. In the garden she weeded through tidy and put some small plants in soil into tomato boxes, ready for re-siting in the new garden.

On the phone to Mary, Ling told her about the bundle of down cushions she had got free of charge and which she hoped to re-cover with the material that Gorse had left over from the curtains.

"I'll leave it now till after the move, I seem to be so busy with packing for moving next week, and now with Sally Anne nearly crawling, at least she's going along on her bottom actually, but she's underfoot all day long."

"It's always the same, they're everywhere once they get on the move. She'll soon walk I expect." Mary replied.

"Yes we were dead lucky with Richard, he more or less pulled himself up with his cot-sides and then walked, never having really crawled."

"Just like his Father Dear, that's exactly what Howard did."

———————

Monday brought Angel on her own in her little Morris Minor. Kitty had had an order for fifty boxes of bedding plants for Leicester market so she had to stay and spend the day ferrying them in. So Howard, Peter and Angel were the workforce who went to Manor Farm to sort out the raspberry site. It was far easier than the strawberry area had been. They chose a shady site screened by a huge hedge from the main road, which lay beyond the new small orchard. It was about two acres and would be strip ploughed as for the strawberries, but less wide strips of soil. Just enough to accommodate single rows of raspberries held in by posts and wire. The posts and wire had been ordered to come during April. That would enable them to complete all the preparation work before haytime, when everyone would be too busy to deal with it.

The three of them were very easy together on this occasion. Angel and Peter chatted happily getting to know each other better now. Howard was always a quiet man when working and he left the two of them as much to themselves as he could. They had taken sandwiches with them and Howard left them to eat theirs while he went home to fetch the tractor and plough, having decided that the soil had dried out enough to be workable.

Peter and Angel found a bale each under the Dutch barn, and sat down to enjoy their lunch. Peter chatted to her trying hard to keep his manner normal and his eyes off her lovely hair. He was determined not to do any more wooing for the present in case he frightened her off again. He talked about his childhood, and his early holidays with the farm people.

"I suppose you could say that I made my home here, after my parents died. I always found a real welcome and so much kindness in Aunt Mary and Uncle John."

"Do you intend to stay around here? Or shall you move on?" Peter hoped he heard just a hint of anxiety in her question.

"Well now I'm on permanent staff at Hill Farm, I can use the skills I have in Uncle John's workshop and they are teaching me all the farm skills as well. I love the life and I think it suits me. I feel so fit, better than I ever did in Coventry."

"I've always liked being outdoors best, that's why I went for horticultural training. My parents have a nursery garden just a few miles into Leicestershire beyond Kitty and Jim's place."

"Do you work full-time for Kitty?"

"I go whenever she needs me but I also help on my parents nursery when Kitty's not so busy. But you didn't really answer my question did you? Shall you move on, perhaps when you've got all the farming skills off pat?" Her eyes questioned him as she spoke.

"Well I think .... that is, in some ways I'd like to stay here forever but I may up and go right away. It all depends." Peter spoke very gently, pouring coffee from his flask as he spoke.

"What does it depend on Peter?" The green eyes looked straight into his.

"I don't think you really want me to answer that just now; and I think you probably know the answer already. How about one of Mary's raspberry turn-overs for afters? I can assure you that they're lovely." Peter offered the open tin to her across the space between them. She smiled and took a turn-over, biting straight into it with her even white teeth. The moment between them passed and he turned the talk back to the farm people. Presently Howard came across the fields with the tractor, under the little railway tunnel. Peter went to set up the plough while Howard ate his sandwiches. After that they took turn and turn about. Afternoon saw the job done. Peter discing behind Howard, with the Ford Dexta from under the barn. Angel turning in the rough edges.

Angel drove Peter back to the farm by car. Howard took the big tractor and plough. When they pulled up in the yard Mary came to the kitchen window, holding the teapot aloft for them to see. Peter got out and went round to the driver's side to open the door for Angel, she slipped quickly out.

"Don't desert me again my Angel .... come soon," he spoke softly.

"I do hope you don't find you have to up and go right away Peter. It is so nice here." She ran away across the yard before he could speak again.

Two days later Angel was working in Kitty's garden, preparing the ground for sowing peas. In the lovely old Queen Anne house Kitty was sorting laundry in the kitchen. Hearing the sound of a car outside the window, she saw the farm car draw up. Somewhat surprised Kitty hurried out to the back door. Peter was getting out of the car. Kitty thought he looked very handsome, hair brushed, neat sports-jacket and flannels over a clean shirt and tie.

"Hello, where did you spring from?"

"I've been sent by Uncle John and Howard, is Angel here by any chance?"

"Yes she is, have you come to carry her off?" Kitty's face was alive with amusement.

"Well no not quite. Borrow her for a few hours. I'm going to the Mayfield works to get the garden tractor and all the attachments. Aunt Mary suggested it actually, and that I should take Angel along because she has so much know-how." Peter gave a huge grin as he explained.

"Aunt Mary indeed. Well, well, Mum's an old matchmaker that's what. Far be it from me to put a spanner into the works of ROMANCE. To say nothing of any scheme your Aunt Mary may be hatching. Feel free to take my right-hand woman. Never mind who plants the peas." Kitty was laughing as she spoke.

"She's planting peas is she? where's the kitchen garden?"

"Feel free, help yourself. Through the garage doors, little door at the back, through there and then turn right past the potting shed." Kitty was already turning back to her laundry. Peter hastened through the garage. The door beyond was open. Turning right he rounded the corner of the potting shed. Without warning Angel stepped out in front of him, she paused and drew in her breath. Peter never stopped to think, he caught hold of her and drew her close in his arms, bending his head until his lips found hers. It was a lingering tender kiss. His hand moved to her hair, cradled her head and mingled in the red curls. She didn't resist him at all, her lips responded at once to his. Her hands moved up into his fair curls. A moment later, he lifted his head.

"Oh Peter, oh it's you," she whispered.

"Yes my Dear Love, and I couldn't have resisted you then if I'd died for it, you know that don't you my Precious?"

"Oh Peter I can't fight you any more, it's as though I'd always known you, as though you'd always been there. Time has nothing to do with it." She rested her head on his shoulder and he kept his arms about her.

"Well I did tell you, you were my Angel, didn't I. I knew it you see, the first moment I saw you."

"But why are you here? I never expected to see you just out of the blue like that."

"Uncle John wants me to take you to help me to buy a Mayfield Tractor and all the implements. That's why I'm here. At least it was when I started out, now I'm not so sure. Oh my lovely Redhead, I'll never let you go again. You know that don't you?"

"Oh Peter that's like a lovely song in my ears, I don't think I can live without you."

"Oh good that's a great blessing, now I'm not going to let myself kiss you again, or we'll be here all morning."

"Peter, I can't go out with you looking like this, old slacks and dirty shirt."

"I think you look sweet, soil on your nose and all, perhaps Kitty will lend you a clean shirt, your trousers are fine. We're going to an oily workplace I expect. Let's ask Kitty about a shirt." They went hand-in-hand to Kitty's kitchen. She looked up from the piles of washing she was sorting on the kitchen floor.

"You still here, all settled is it now?"

"Let's just say I'm a very happy man, can you lend Angel a clean shirt?"

"With pleasure, and the bathroom by the look of it. Top drawer in our bedroom, choose which you like, we're much of a size, hanky's, same drawer but you don't look as if you need one of those today." Angel vanished up the back stairs.

"Ain't Love grand eh Peter?" Kitty was looking delighted.

"Wonderful, I couldn't have asked for more, I haven't a thing to offer her but I intend to marry her the first possible minute."

"What you are offering her is the best thing in the world. The love of one of the Radford men. It's the very best thing I've ever had Peter, and we started with nothing."

"What a marvellous thing to say Kitty, I shall tell Jim when I see him."

"You needn't, he knows." Was the smiling reply.

———————

STRAWBERRIES AND CREAM

Chapter 7

It Never Rains But It Pours

STRAWBERRIES AND CREAM

Chapter 7

It Never Rains But It Pours

It poured with rain all day long on the day that Howard and Ling had planned to move to Manor Farm. As the removal van was a local one from Banworth, Howard rang them in the early morning, on seeing the steady downpour from the bedroom window. They agreed to defer it until the following day. In a way it was helpful to Howard and to Ling, it gave them a day when the farm work was at a standstill, to finish packing, and borrow the farm car so that they could move a lot of personal treasures, the children's toys, clothes and all the china. They spent most of the day organising the kitchen at Manor Farm, and sorting out the smaller pantry beyond. All Ling's bottled fruit, tinned food, jams and pickles were set out on the newly scrubbed shelves. The airing cupboard was stocked with the new and older linen and towels. The china was put away in the kitchen cupboards. In all they had a very happy day. In the early afternoon the telephone people came and re-connected the phone, helped by Richard who thoroughly enjoyed their visit, especially picking up the phone when they tested the instrument afterwards. Ling at once phoned the farm to speak to Mary. As it turned out John answered.

"I just wanted to tell you that our number is Banworth 327, and to say 'Hello' from Manor Farm."

What a day Lass, do you realise that your number is the same as ours except for one digit. Ours is 317. Anyway I'm just writing it in on our number chart by the phone here. Mary's gone into Banworth, it was too wet to do anything outside, so Angel came over in her little car, and they've gone into the shops, trying to be back by six they said. Pete and I are working in the workshop, I only heard the phone because I came in to make a cup of tea. I'll switch the phone over to the workshop when we stop talking."

"OK Dad let's hope the rain stops tomorrow when the real move is on. I'll go now, bye bye."

"Just before you go Lass, tell Howard leave the car till morning, bring it when he comes for his can of milk."

"OK thanks Dad, bye." Ling rang off and rejoined Howard and the children.

"I don't like this rain, the wind's getting up as well and it's still pouring." Howard had been round upstairs making sure that no rain was getting in through roof or windows.

"Actually I wondered if we should stay here, we could but we've no food." Howard didn't like taking the children through such heavy rain.

"Let's stay, I'll make the spare room bed up, everything's ready. Sally Anne can sleep with us, I can do the little bed next door for Richard, be fun won't it Richard?" Ling reassured the children.

"But can you pop and get some bread, butter and milk from the village shop? We've brought over two dozen eggs this morning, here take my umbrella, it got popped in the back of the car along with all the clobber this morning." Howard took a carrier bag, put his already wet mac on and went out into the downpour under Ling's umbrella. Although it was only four o'clock it was already nearly dusk outside and he had to cross the main road carefully.

Ling laid a cloth and put the kettle on and began to get tea. So after all it was going to be their first night in the new house.

On that same afternoon at four-thirty Mary and Angel finished their shopping in Banworth. Both wore macs and waterproof hats against the rain.

"Let's get a pot of tea in the tea-shop Dear, it will fortify you for the drive home. There won't be many in the tea-shop being such a wet day. We'll be served quickly." Mary moved along the pavement as she spoke.

"Yes let's. I feel like a drowned rat. Never mind I've got Kitty's things and some things I've been trying to get time to buy for weeks." They reached the tea-shop and almost fell into the warmth and comfort inside. As Mary had guessed, there was only one other table occupied. Mary pulled off her mac and sou'wester and hung them over an empty chair.

"What a day, it's never stopped since early morning."

"I know, it's a blessing the men have finished sowing the corn. Ah here's our tea coming, a hot cuppa is just what I need." Mary poured and they each had a scone off the trolley. It was five-fifteen when they left the shop and hurried back to the car which was parked in the Swan yard. Angel lifted their bags into the boot and helped Mary into the front seat.

"I must take this old hat off it stifles me." Mary threw her hat down behind the front seat. Angel climbed into the driver's seat and soon they were moving out of the yard. The rain beat down on the windscreen and it was all the wipers could do to keep it clear enough for Angel to see her way. Once on the main road it was easier. There was little traffic but it was almost dark.

"Just go very steady Dear, John's not expecting us before six. I dare say he and Peter will have milked a bit early and put the tea on for us. They often do if I've been out."

"Not much traffic Mrs. Radford, but this rain is so heavy I shall have to go slow."

"Never mind the Mrs. Radford Lass, either Mary or Aunt Mary will do me fine. Am I right in thinking we may be related soon? Not to be a nosy old woman, but our Peter's looked that happy these last days."

"Yes, yes we are happy but that's all at the moment it's not long since we realised and we want to hold on to the newness of it all just for a little longer." Angel smiled in the darkness. It seemed an endless journey to Mary and she only made an occasional encouraging remark to Angel. She felt very worried about Angel having to drive in such conditions. She spent most of the journey peering out over the fields looking for landmarks. After the village cross-roads, there was two miles of twisting main road, then past the tiny lane which led to Bunny Warren. Two hundred yards beyond would be the turning left into their own Hill Farm lane. Mary strained her eyes to see the cottage lane, and at last picked it out from the car's head-lights.

"Very slow Dear, our bend is two hundred yards along on the left. You'll see a big tree." Mary's remark probably saved her life. Angel slowed down to a crawl, looking for the tree. Without warning, lights blazed on them and round the bend a big vehicle, Mary thought it was a lorry, hurtled almost in their path. The vehicle literally pushed them off the road and both women felt the car shake and tip, then the most almighty crash and the sound of tearing metal and breaking glass. Mary seemed to feel herself lifted and then falling, and as she fell twigs and branches scratched her head and face. Then they hit the hedge. Mary could still hear the big vehicle thundering off up the road. Their own engine was silent, then a terrible wave of faintness swept over Mary. She put out her hand and felt for Angel, found her sleeve and gripped it.

"Are you all right Lass, oh my Deary are you all right?"

"Yes, yes I think so, but my legs are stuck, the doors on me. And I think my face is cut. But I'm all right. Oh Mary are you all right?" Angel's voice shook and Mary could hear her sobbing with shock.

"Now Lass that other vehicle's not stopped, I'm going to see if I can get out. It's only ten minutes up the lane. I don't think I'm hurt but you'll have to be very brave Lass and just wait quietly in the dark. Shall you be all right if I try?"

"Yes I'll be fine but it's wet, will you be able to get there?"

"Yes surely Love, but first let's see if I can get out." Mary tried her door and found it opened but only half-way. Could she get through? She pushed and pushed but it wouldn't budge an inch. Perhaps if she twisted round. Come on woman, the voice inside her head grumbled at her. No messing, Angel's got to have help, and you've got to get it for her. Bracing herself with both arms she pushed herself upwards until her head and shoulders were through the gap between door and roof. "Oh bugger these big-busted women!" The voice in her head muttered. That had always been a little private joke between her and John. Was it John's voice in her head? Push! Push! Push, said the voice firmly. Suddenly she was free but she seemed to be sitting half on the car roof and half in the hedge. The thorns tore at her through her clothes. Now Mary, the firm voice again, slide down onto the bonnet, mind the glass. At last she was lying on the grass. Again faintness overcame her, so nice to just lie here with the rain on her face. Get up! Get up! You have to get home. She pulled herself up by the front of the car which seemed to be above her. The lane, where was the lane? She must stand up! Now get across the grass. She turned her ankle in a hole and almost fell. None of that you fool! The voice again. Come on Lass, walk, walk, easy now, good girl, keep steady. Surely she would fall, no she mustn't fall. Up the lane. It was still raining she could feel the wet on her face. If only she had a hanky, she'd left it in her bag in the car. If only John had put the outside light on for them coming. She felt herself stumble, no she must not fall, must not fall. A field gate came into her vision. Thank God, the front field gate. She was over half way. What had happened to her glasses, no wonder she couldn't see properly? Please God let the light be on. Then she saw it, just a faint flicker in the darkness, but it was there. The voice was at her again. Well done Mary! Nearly there, the garden wall. She leant against it for a moment and was suddenly very sick. Oh God, there was her scone and two cups of tea all over the road! Better up than down! Was it Granny used to say that? Stop fussing woman, what the bloody hell does it matter who said it? Don't stand idling here, get up the yard! Get help for Angel. She put out her hand and clung to the farmyard gatepost. Forced herself to let go and take painful steps up the stony yard, she felt herself swaying from side to side. The rain beating down in front of the yard lights seemed to tilt the house and buildings towards her. she mustn't faint now, she simply must not faint now. At last the kitchen window. Just a few steps to the latch, where was the latch? Ah under her hand. She put all her weight against the door and pressed the latch.

John in the kitchen heard the door, and worried because the time was well turned half-past-six, moved quickly towards it. It flew open and Mary fell into his arms.

"Oh John, oh John Love," she said and fainted.

"Quick Peter, help me," Peter rushed from the sitting room.

"Oh my God. Wait a bit, pull my big chair," they man-handled her across the kitchen and into the big chair, but she was already coming round.

"Car .... accident, bottom of our lane. Angel can't get out. Something hit us, didn't stop. Oh John I never thought I'd get to you. Peter go and see, but please, please don't leave me John."

"No Darling Lass, I'm here, I'll see to you in a minute. Now Pete we've got to keep calm. Ring Howard, he's likely at Manor Farm still, new number is on the pad. Tell him to get the police and an ambulance to the end of our road, Banworth road end and then bring the car here. Then take a blanket .... in the airing cupboard, and bring the lambing torch and go and see after your Angel. I'll see to Mary here." Peter had reached the phone before John finished speaking. Seconds later Howard's voice came on the line.

"Howard," the urgency in Peter's voice made Howard's hand tighten on the phone.

"Yes I'm here what is it?"

"Accident with Angel's car, on the bend, bottom of our lane. Aunt Mary's got back here very shocked. Can you get an ambulance and the police? I'm going down the lane. Angel's trapped in the car."

"OK, ring off Pete, tell Dad we'll be with him in fifteen minutes." Peter was on the stairs, he grabbed a blanket off the shelf and was back in the kitchen within seconds.

"Take Howard's lambing mack, behind the door, lights on the

ledge," John never looked up from his care of Mary.

"Tell him to take a hammer, he may be able to get the door off." Whispered Mary.

"Yes Lad, a hammer, on the workshop window sill." Peter threw on the waterproof coat and grabbed the light. The workshop door opened to his touch. The rack of tools held wrenches, tyre levers and hammers. He took all three, and legs pumping set off down the yard. He had the blanket folded tight under his coat, but that needed a hand to keep it there. As he ran down the yard he saw an old sack by the gatepost, pausing to get it, he pushed the tools inside and ran on into the lane. His feet thudded as he ran. The rain was beating on his face. His heart pounded to the prayer in his heart.

"Let her be all right, let her be safe, please, please don't take her from me." That terrible run down the lane was to live with him for the rest of his life. It seemed such a distance. The tools clanking in the sack. The light bobbing up and down in front of him, and the terrible grinding fear in the pit of his stomach. His own rasping breath, and worst of all his legs pumping away and yet the feeling that he was being so slow. That the rain was actually pinning him back and keeping him away from her.

At last he reached the first bend, not far now. What if she was already .... and he'd never told her they would be married. He felt the rain mingling with tears on his cheeks. But he was nearly there. He swung the light towards the right-hand hedge and suddenly saw the car. It was in total darkness but a small wave of hope came to him. The front end was tipped into the hedge and ditch. How on earth had Mary got out? But the bonnet looked undamaged, and the driver's door was only slightly dented. The back looked as though smashed in by a giant hammer. He was on the grass at last, swinging the light round to the driving seat. Angel was inside, her head forward over the steering-wheel, her hands still gripping the sides of the wheel, her one arm jammed down tight against the door. There was glass everywhere. Half the driver's window was gone. He put his hand in carefully through the broken glass.

"I'm here Darling, it's Peter." His hand found hers on the wheel and held it fast.

"Soon have you out of there." Her fingers felt cold but not lifeless, they closed a little on his. He drew a huge breath of relief. He released her fingers and lifted her head, her face was covered in blood but she opened her eyes to the light.

"Oh Peter, see to Mary, I'm all right, just got my feet stuck under the pedals and my arm hurts too, but Mary, she hasn't spoken for ages. Peter she's not ...."

"No Darling she's fine, she made it up to the farm to Uncle John. And Howard and Ling are coming there too. Now let's see if we can get you more comfortable. The ambulance is on its way and the police. I'm just the advance guard. I'm not going to try forcing the door. I'll come in with you from Mary's seat. I've got a rug Darling we'll pick the glass off you and wrap you up a bit warmer. Does your head feel all right?" She nodded.

"Thank God for that, we've got to take great care of that lovely hair haven't we Dearest? Hold on a sec while I get in." He climbed on up over the bonnet and let himself in through the narrow space allowed by the half open passenger door.

"My God this is a tight go, how in hell did Mary get out, it must have been terrible?" Seconds later he was in the seat beside her, picking the slivers of glass off her clothes and out of her hair, throwing them through the broken window and all the time talking to her,

"Now Love that's better I'm not going to touch your face, you've a few cuts on your lovely cheeks. I'm going to try to wrap you up in this blanket." He lifted her hair and passed the end of the blanket across her back.

"Now your arm Darling, is it jammed against the door? Or can you move it forward a little bit?" Angel tried with a great effort to move her arm.

I think it's the elbow, that's where it hurts, down against the door."

"Let me try, if we could lift it a bit I could get the blanket under and the other end can wrap round across your lap. Thank

110

goodness it's stopped raining at last, you were getting soaked through that broken window. Shout if I hurt." He took her arm in both his hands and tenderly eased it upwards and across her lap. She gasped twice but did not cry out. He heard the broken glass fall down into the car and picked the remainder from her sleeve. Then he eased the blanket round tucking it down round her legs. All this with the lamp perched on the dashboard. He took her good hand in his own and kissed it gently.

"Oh my Dear Love, just a few more minutes, now I'm going to get out again and see if I can get that door open." It was easier said than done, and again he realised the miracle of Mary having got through the narrow gap. Round by the door again, he reached for the tool bag in the grass. Thank God for the tyre lever, it was the very thing. He leant in and pushed the lever between the side of the seat and the door, twisting it round seeking some purchase to wrench it hard enough. Then he heaved with all his strength. The door burst outwards scattering the last of the broken window glass into the grass. He moved the light to a better angle and pushed a dead tree branch against the door to keep it wide open.

"There Darling, that's better isn't it?"

"Peter I'm so glad you came. I thought I was going to die. Those huge lights. I think it was a lorry, right in front of us, the car seemed to stand on end. Then nothing, just silence, I think Mary spoke to me once but I can't remember, are you sure she's all right, you're not just telling me that are you?" Tears were running down her face. His hand caressed her hair as his voice soothed her.

"Mary's fine Dearest, and you'll be fine, I can hear the ambulance bell now. Let me say, as soon as you are well we shall be married. I shall ask Mary and John for Bunny Warren for us. You will marry me won't you my Treasure?"

"Yes, yes I'd love that, as soon as we can." A moment later police car and ambulance were on the scene. At once an efficient caring service took complete charge. Peter stood back.

"This way George, bring the stretcher, her feet are trapped, brake pedal jammed I shouldn't wonder. See if you can shift it. If I shove a pad in to protect her feet. That's it now try. Now Miss don't you make no effort. I'll lift your feet. Tell me first have you pain? Where do you hurt?"

"It's my arm, Peter managed to get it across my lap."

"Good work. Just one feel at that elbow Miss, sorry." As Angel cried out. "There now it's broken I'm afraid. Get me a wrap round sling George will you? I'm just going to tie your arm in, it will hurt until it's set at the hospital, I expect, but you'll travel more comfortable with a sling." He eased her arm up to slip the sling under and secured the ends around her neck.

"No pain in your back or neck Love have you?"

"No just my feet, I can't move them."

"Have a go at these pedals George."

"Would this tyre lever help, that's how I got the door open, it was jammed against her arm?" Peter passed the tyre lever to George.

"Just the job, here George, I've got the pad across her feet. See if you can ram the pedals up." George heaved.

"Easy as cutting butter. Can you lift her legs out?"

"A few minutes later Angel was lying on the stretcher with blankets tucked around her. Peter gave a sigh of relief and turned to the two policemen who were wanting details of all Peter knew about the accident. He told them only briefly and then ran to get in the ambulance.

"Are you a relative?" Asked George.

"Going to be her husband as soon as possible." replied Peter with a grim smile.

"OK jump in." Said George.

"We'll go up the farm and see the other lady, as soon as we've measured up here. Have to talk to you and the young lady tomorrow maybe." The sergeant spoke very kindly. then the ambulance door closed and they were on the road heading for Banworth Hospital.

———————

112

At Hill Farm after Peter's departure, John just held Mary in his arms for several minutes.

"I think I'm going to be sick again." She whispered.

"Half a tick, I'll get a bowl." He held her head while she heaved again.

"Didn't think there could be anything left after I threw up in the lane." A wan smile came and went. "Better now Dear, but don't leave me Love."

"Let me take this away and get some clean water to sponge your hands and face, then a glass of brandy perhaps." John moved quietly about the kitchen.

"Rather have a cup of tea Darling."

"All right, kettle won't be long and I'm doing you a hot water bottle as well." Just at that moment Ling burst in through the back door followed by Howard with the child asleep in his arms. Behind came little Richard white-faced. Ling took in the whole situation at a glance.

"Just pop Sally Anne in bed Howard. Richard Darling Nanny's all right she's just been a bit hurted, like you are sometimes. Mummy and Grandad will mend her carefully and you pop up to bed with Daddy and see her in the morning." Richard took one wide-eyed look at Mary and ran up the stairs.

"He'll be fine with Howard." Ling spoke reassuringly.

"Here Dad let me do that," she carried the basin of warm water and flannel to the kitchen table and began to gently sponge the blood and glass fragments off Mary's face.

"She came up the lane like that. God knows how." Suddenly John looked at breaking point.

"Make us some tea Dad, and put plenty of sugar for you and Mum." John moved to do her bidding, his hand shaking on the kettle handle. Ling, calm and steady continued sponging and patting dry.

"There my Dear Mum, you'll soon be as good as new." She planted a little kiss on Mary's uninjured cheek.

"It's my legs Lass, I think they're just jelly, no strength left, oh how silly." Tears welled up and ran down her cheeks.

"Never mind Pet, never mind. Here's a cup of hot tea coming can you hold it? There best take it slow, just sips. It'll do you the world of good. Ah there you are Howard, could you go back up and bring your Mum's dressing gown and slippers and a clean warm nightgown? In the top drawer are they Mum?"

"Yes Dear, pink with long sleeves." Howard turned away and headed upstairs again collecting the things Ling had asked for, peeping in on the children as he passed. Sally Anne was still sleeping peacefully. Richard, huge-eyed, lay in the half-light.

"Is Nanny nearly mended Daddy?"

"Yes son I'm taking her nightie down and slippers so your Mummy can make her comfy. I'll come up and see you again soon."

In the kitchen Ling shooed the men out.

"I'll get her undressed and comfortable and then she can come through on the settee and have a lie down. Two of those cuts may need a stitch, I think we should ring the Doctor, I'm sure he should see her tonight, anyway could you make up a nice fire and find some pillows and a blanket for the settee?"

"I'll see to it Dad," Howard felt anxious about John. He had never seen his Father look so drawn and strained.

"You sit and drink your tea, I've done the fire, then you can be here for Mum when she comes through."

In the kitchen Mary was being gently peeled out of her wet clothes. She was still weeping a little and shaking at times. Ling warmed her nightgown in front of the Aga and slipped it over her head.

"There now Mum, you can peel off your corsets and knicks nice and private. I'll help you, just stand up and step out of them. That's it. Now your dressing gown and slippers. Here put this towel under your feet, there's bits of glass all over, we'll have to have a broom up later." To Mary the comfort of the warm loose nightgown coupled with Ling's calm steady care of her, and the touch of her gentle hands, did more to push away remembered details of the dreadful evening than anything else could have done. Ling put her head round the sitting room door.

"Now if you help me with your Mum. We'll see if we can get her on the settee." Howard took up position one side of Mary, Ling the other, he slipped his arm under Mary's and across her back.

"There we go Mum, put your weight on me, I'm a strong Lad you know." Mary moved slowly forward and once alongside the settee it was plain sailing. Mary sank back into the pillows and closed her eyes. Howard lifted her feet up along the settee. Ling tucked blankets and hot water bottle in cosy and sat down to watch over her patient anxiously. Mary's face was colourless except the slight scarlet escape of blood from two gashes in her right cheek.

"What about the doctor?" Ling turned to Howard.

"He'll be here in about half an hour."

"I can't see her going upstairs tonight can you?"

"I want to be with John," Mary's eyes opened and lit up when she saw John sitting in his armchair opposite.

"So you shall my Love, I'll put the armchairs together and stop down here with you. I can keep the fire up and make a cuppa when we want. These two youngsters can climb the stairs tonight and sleep in our bed." John smiled across at his wife and she closed her eyes and sank back in relief. At that moment a knock came on the back door and the phone rang.

"I'll get the phone if you'll do the door." Ling went through to the hall and Howard was met at the door by two policemen. He invited them in and sat them down at the kitchen table, while he explained everything as far as he knew it.

"And does the young man, Peter I think he said his name was, does he live here?"

"Oh yes he's my cousin, lives in .... when my Mother more or less collapsed in the doorway, Dad saw to her, Peter phoned me to get police and ambulance, and then he ran down the road to see to Angel."

"Did you say Angel sir?"

"Yes that's right, Angela she is really, but everyone calls her Angel. And for Peter, well you could say she is the only one!"

115

"Well I should say Angel or not, an Angel was looking after her tonight. Whatever came round that corner nearly took the side off that little Morris Minor. We shall do a proper examination on site tomorrow and need to talk to your Mother. Can I see her? No need to talk. Has the doctor seen her?"

"Coming in a few minutes, just put your head round the door, my wife's got her undressed and onto the settee." The police sergeant peered round the door, took one look at Mary's white face and withdrew.

"Poor lady, I'm glad the Doctor's coming. We'll get along now and see you in the morning."

In the hall Ling was on the phone.

"She's going to be all right. I wanted to ring straight away in case Aunt Mary was worried. She's got lacerations to her hands and face, and a broken right arm. But she looks so much better now she's all cleaned up and in bed."

"What about you Peter, are you OK, you sound done in?"

"I suppose I am but I'm so bloody thankful she's all in one piece. We're going to be married the first moment I can get her out of here.

"Well done, Howard and I will both be delighted you know. Are you staying at the hospital tonight?"

"Yes there's a room where I can lie down, I can't leave her Ling, but tell your Dad I'll be there to milk in the morning. He's had a dreadful shock, your Dad has."

"I know, but don't fret over milking, Howard and I are staying here, several days probably, we'll see how Mum goes on. She's very shocked, but undressed and resting on the settee. Doctor's coming any minute, Howard's got the police in the kitchen at the moment."

"Poor Aunt Mary, how she got out of that car and came all up the lane, I shall never know, I could hardly get in beside Angel the way Mary got out. The passenger door was jammed more than half-shut and the car nearly up-ended."

"Never mind Love, they are both still alive, and we can only thank God from the bottom of our hearts for it. Anyway we'll see you in the morning."

Back in the sitting room Mary opened her eyes, anxiety writ large in them.

"Who was on the phone?"

"Peter Mum, now don't fret, Angel's OK, she's got cuts like you and a broken arm, but she'll mend. Peter's stopping with her tonight at the hospital, and as soon as she's well enough they are getting married. How does that appeal to you then?" Ling smiled for the first time that evening. Mary's eyes met John's,

"Oh John we'll have another wedding, think of that, I'm so happy." Tears streamed down her face and she was still mopping up in John's hanky when the Doctor came in with Howard a few minutes later. He examined her carefully asking gentle questions all the time.

"I must put a stitch or two in those cuts but otherwise you've had a lucky escape." He opened his bag and took out what he needed, his neat fingers and kindly way, and the fact that she knew him from times past reassured Mary. He put one stitch in the small cut and two into the larger gash.

"There now, stop on the settee down here tonight will you? Plenty of hot drinks. cry as much as you like, helps carry away the strain out of you. John'll mind you, and the young ones, are they staying overnight?"

"Yes Doctor we'll stay a few days and keep Mum off her feet." Ling smiled at him.

"Good girl, this is bound to knock the stuffing out of her for a bit. I've seen the young lady at the hospital, she was in the same accident wasn't she? Is she to do with you? Lovely red hair anyway. Wasn't it young Peter down there with her?"

"Yes it was. And Peter thinks her hair's lovely too. In fact we're going to have another wedding Doctor."

"Oh yes. Well that'll buck up Mary Radford, if I know anything about it." The Doctor looked down at Mary while he re-packed his bag.

"Oh yes," Mary's tears fell again, "it's nothing, just that I'm so happy about Peter and Angel." Mary dashed the tears away with a watery smile.

"Well you could've fooled me, anyway I shall pop in on you tomorrow just to keep an eye. Goodnight to you all." and he was on his way. Soon afterwards Howard and Ling went up to bed in John and Mary's bed. John and Mary settled down by the fire. John felt dead tired. Mary felt as though her body belonged to someone else and that all the aches and pains she felt were nothing to do with her. She was just glad to lie back and drop into sleep. They woke in the night, Mary needed the toilet. With John's help she found she could get to the little outside toilet by the back door.

John made up the fire and made a hot cup of tea. He was thankful to see her so much improved.

"I couldn't live without you my Lass, you know that don't you?"

"Oh John we are so lucky to have each other." She replied.

"Now Love cuddle down and get back to sleep. It's doing you so much good, just to sleep." He tucked the blanket up to her chin and kissed her gently, drawing away to look into her face. More colour now, praise be, he thought thankfully. Her eyes flew open.

"D'you know John I've had such a good idea. Peter and Angel could have Bunny Warren. To live I mean. Wouldn't it be lovely?"

"Now I know you're mending my Love, get to sleep now.

STRAWBERRIES AND CREAM

Chapter 8

Moving In

STRAWBERRIES AND CREAM

Chapter 8

Moving In

In the morning the rain had stopped and the sun came out as if to deny the disaster of the previous day. Howard got up early and had nearly finished milking, with young Bill, when Peter came up the yard on a borrowed bicycle. He was unshaven and weary, having been awake for most of the night at the hospital. In the house Ling was in charge, the children and John sitting at their breakfast. Mary after a disturbed night had been helped up to her own bed for a good sleep. Ling took up a vase of daffodils from the garden. She also took up a tray of tea and toast with a boiled egg, Mary's favourite breakfast.

Ling who was cooking Howard's and young Bill's breakfasts, at once added more eggs to the pan and sat Peter down to a mug of hot tea and a plateful of eggs and bacon.

"Then I think you ought to get a few hours sleep. We are getting back to normal but no real work is to be done today. Everyone's too weary. Mum's hoping to come down later but take things quietly. I'm doing meals and poultry here and the two children are staying with me. Howard's going ahead with the move to Manor Farm, we've put the men off once already. Everything's packed ready, we've moved all the small things, so Howard's going along to Bunny Warren at eleven o'clock to meet the men. Young Bill says he can manage the yard work here. I can manage the hens. So you could get a sleep." Peter was enjoying his food.

"Well, why don't I sleep a couple of hours and then get up and give Howard a hand at the cottage? Only thing is, I do want to get over to the hospital again this afternoon to see Angel."

"Surely, Kitty's coming over to take charge here while I go to see Angel after dinner. If I come with you we could take Dad's car. Could we Dad?"

"Yes Lass but Peter may want to stay longer." John looked up from his toast with a smile.

"No I thought, if I came back and helped Bill milk, Howard can see the furniture in and concentrate on the move. Then I could go to the hospital again this evening when no one's going. Angel's Dad and Mum are with her this morning and she's coming on fine."

"Mary is too. The police think we've been very lucky. Have they moved the car yet?"

"No the police are still taking pictures in case they can catch the driver of the other vehicle. I think they hope to move it tomorrow."

"I'll be glad when it's gone, I wouldn't like either Aunt Mary or Angel to see it again."

"Well Angel won't be home yet and Mum's not going to get that far for a while." Richard's serious little face looked up from his food.

"If they catch that man Mummy, will he have to say sorry to my Nanny, for making her so hurted?"

"Well Darling I think the policeman will tell him he can't drive anymore." Ling smiled gently down at Richard.

"Well that's good then he can't hurted anyone else's Nanny. Can I have a drink please?" Peter finished eating and went up the stairs in a very tired but thankful frame of mind.

Howard and Bill came in and had their breakfast. The two children played in the sitting room. John after checking that Mary was asleep decided to have a walk across the fields towards Manor Farm. He felt he needed some fresh air but did not feel up to anything much in the way of work. Even the workshop with his welding which usually soothed him, seemed too much effort today. As he walked down the front fields, he turned and looked back towards Hill Farmhouse, his eyes drawn to the bedroom window. He had been born in that room. All his three sons had been born in that big bed. At this moment Mary, his dearly beloved Mary, his Love, his wife, his best friend, lay sleeping there. She could so easily have been dead. he turned away and went on down towards the little tunnel under the railway. And as he walked he wept. He had not wept for years. Once through the tunnel he was in the small field that he and Howard had sown a few weeks before. He walked on along the hedge-line into the next field. This was the field that Howard had already named the Mound Field. John climbed the tiny hill. Birds were singing in the trees and warm sun was opening the buds of two primrose plants in the bank. On the top he was surprised how far he could see. Across the reservoir where the swans were nesting, and wild ducks on the water were about their daily chores. He could see all Hill Farm's front fields. Looking the other way he could see all the building complex at Manor Farm, the lovely old farmhouse, Ling's new garden, where he could imagine her working, and the children calling to one another as they played. To the right and left, were spread the Manor Farm fields. Howard's fields. How good it all looked. He pulled out his pipe, filled it and lit it and as he puffed away, he drank in the joy of all he could see, and serenity returned to him. Mary was alive, and they would be together to enjoy the fun of Howard and Ling's new farm. God was so good. Howard was moving in today. John turned to walk back to Hill Farm. Now Mary might be awake again.

————————

At Hill Farm the day went quickly by. Everyone was filled with a deep feeling of thankfulness, and through that, they also felt great goodwill one with another. Rev. Cost the vicar, hearing of the accident, came and spent an hour with Mary and John. Ling arranged, and cooked meals, collected eggs, made tea, spent time with Mary and went to see Angel. Everything went smoothly and quietly. Mary rather shakily got dressed before dinner and sat for a while by the sitting room fire with John.

In contrast, at Bunny Warren life was hectic. The removal van arrived on time at eleven o'clock. There were three men with the van. They began to load up quickly and efficiently. Howard and Peter swept up after them and cleaned the bathroom and kitchen. When the house was clear, Howard picked up the little stone rabbit; the garden seat was already on the van, and wrapped him in newspaper and put him in a carrier bag. Lings plants were also in the van in boxes on the back of the load. The men drove off and it was suddenly very quiet. The birds were singing, daffodils and wallflowers in full flower.

"Glad Ling couldn't be here, she would have been upset, she loved it so." Howard glanced into the deserted rooms.

"Well you've most generously left the curtains and stair carpet, someone may come before you know it." Peter's eyes twinkled as he spoke. Howard's mind was on other things.

"Let's get up to the farm to dinner. The men will come to unload at Manor Farm at half past two, they're going to the Plough pub on the green at Brushstoke for their dinner. I want to be at the new house before then. Howard locked the cottage door and taking the key with him to leave at Hill Farm, they got in the farm car, which they had parked along Bunny Warren lane, and went home. They were thankful to see that Angel's car had been removed from the scene of the crash. All that remained was the shattered hedge and bank disturbance on the corner.

At Hill Farm dinner was a rich meaty stew which Mary had prepared before going out the day before. That time now seemed ages ago. Ling had done extra potatoes and carrots and a creamy rice pudding for afters. When the meal was finished and cleared; Mary and John had had theirs on plates by the fireside, Ling and Howard did the dishes before Kitty arrived in her car, ready to housekeep while Ling went with Peter to see Angel. Peter drove them in Kitty's car, leaving the farm car free for Howard to go to Brushstoke. The two cars set off at quarter to two, taking the same route past the station until Howard, lifting his hand in farewell, turned left for Brushstoke. He was early, but only a few minutes before the men got there with the van. They, like the previous van, decided to unload from the yard by the kitchen. Howard had time to put more fuel on the Aga and riddle the ashes. He then set the kettle on the slow plate. He knew that Ling had wanted to be with him and share in the move in, so he was determined to make it all look as nice for her as he possibly could.

The men came in with the carpets which had been put in last.

"We've put the garden seat and them boxes of plants in the rear garden Gov."

"Thanks, that's great. Let's get the carpets down, the big one goes in the far sitting room, the others are bedrooms, except the green one. That goes in the little room at the back, the office."

The carpets were quickly laid and the furniture set in place. When all was done Howard made a big pot of tea and cut slabs of fruit cake, left ready by Ling. He saw the men away with an extra few pounds in their pockets and went back into the house. It was half past three, he could have an hour and a half, or even two hours. He piled the mugs in the sink and washed them clean. Then he went from room to room making tidy, unpacking books, children's toys, the sitting room clock, favourite ornaments, cushions, and clothes. These last he hung in wardrobes and folded in drawers. He spent half an hour sorting beds. The bed they'd made up in the spare room the day before, thinking to stay, but abandoned because of the accident, had to be dismantled. Their own big bed from the cottage was now in their own room in position. In the spare room he pulled off all the bedding and left the bed with only neat folded blankets, pillows and a new cream bedspread on top. Instead he made up their own bed and turned the covers back ready for night. Sally Anne's nursery cot was made up fresh, her toys put out and her rocking horse put in the corner of her little room. Richard's room next Howard decided. The little brass bed was ready and he placed Richard's teddies at the end. His little clock with ducks on the side went on the shelf. His books in the bookshelf and his little cars set out on the wide window sill. All his toys were put into his cupboard and his favourite, rather worn red rug was unrolled by the bed. No more need be done in the house, Howard decided. Pictures and mirrors were stacked in the far sitting room. They would put those up later when Ling was here to choose. He looked at the clock, newly sited on the sitting room mantle-piece. It was time to get back to the farm to help with cows and stock. He knew how knocked out his Father was feeling today. But just a few minutes in the garden. He put the boxes of plants on the path by the wall ready for Ling to plant them. The seat he carried and put near the snowdrops and the nut bush, which was hung all over with yellow catkins. There were clumps of yellow daffodils everywhere. Howard's heart lifted to see them. Ling would quickly learn to love this garden. In the old may tree in a niche in the trunk was a newly built wrens nest. The wren was already sitting on her eggs, and she flew off into the lilac bush as Howard went past with the seat.

He did not put out the little stone rabbit. Back in the kitchen he unwrapped, and sat the bunny on the middle of the table ready to welcome Ling when she came home.

At Hill Farm life was returning to normal. After milking, tea was laid for everyone on the kitchen table. Ling had made a big fresh sponge cake during milking. She filled it with layers of home-made raspberry jam and whipped thick Jersey cream. There were plates of brown and white bread and butter, ham and a good wedge of cheese, and chocolate biscuits for the children. Everyone sat round the table. Mary hobbled in from the sitting room, her legs almost back to full use. Her biggest problem, not the stitches in her face, which she could hardly feel, but her ankle which she had wrenched in a hole in the grass down the lane.

The conversation at tea-time was mostly centred on Angel. It was expected that she would be unable to come home for ten days or so. Peter was going to see her again after tea, taking a bunch of flowers from Mary's garden. It was decided that

Howard and his family would go home to Manor Farm for the night, but for the next few days Ling would come daily to do the dinner for them all at Hill Farm. Bill had taken over the poultry, although Mary had insisted that she would wash the eggs, and have a walk round down the orchard from tomorrow morning on. The mens minds were turning back to field-work again, there were several contract jobs waiting to be done. At home rolling and harrowing the grass fields was next on the agenda. John intended to make a start on it the following day. The flock of ewes and lambs were to be moved across to Manor Farm pastures to be close at hand for Howard's watchful eyes. The fields they vacated would be spread with fertilizer and shut up to grow on ready for hay.

Mary's mind was on her next batch of chickens, due by rail at Banworth station in a weeks time.

"Perhaps you could spare me Bill one day this week John? To clear the pen and disinfect it, so I can set up the lamps and the chick hoover in readiness."

"Yes Love but you let young Bill tackle most of the hard slog, I don't want you to get doing too much for a week or two."

It was dusk when Howard and Ling and their children came home to Manor Farm, that first evening. Howard switched on the yard light as they went in through the kitchen door.

"Oh Mummy there's our bunny from home, is he coming to live here too?" Richard reached across the kitchen table to touch the stone rabbit.

"Yes, we are too fond of him to leave him behind. He's part of the family. Mummy will choose where to put him in the garden, when it's daylight." Howard explained.

"Oh Howard, he was sitting on the table waiting for us, how lovely." Ling turned and laid her hand on Howard's arm.

"We shall soon feel at home. The flock with all our lambs will be here in our fields tomorrow and the builder is coming next week to start converting the stable into the Farm Shop. We can start on our own work here and organise the tearoom. We shall have to get down to it, if we hope to open both shop and tearoom for Easter."

"Are we going to use this kitchen for a tearoom or the sitting room? Which do you think?" Ling was looking round and visualising the room with small tables and all the Windsor chairs round them.

"Well let's get these two scraps into bed, then we can make a nightcap drink and discuss it." Sally Anne was nearly asleep on her Father's shoulder. They took the children upstairs and as every light switch was turned on Ling exclaimed at how homely and welcoming Howard had managed to make the house. Ling undressed Sally Anne and sponged her face. Five minutes later she was lying down in her cot with Dollyblob who was a special old favourite rag doll. Richard ran round and looked in all the bedrooms, then quite satisfied that this was now home, allowed himself to be helped with toilet and pyjamas.

"I like my new bobbly bed, it's so long, I can reach my legs right down and still not touch the end." He said proudly.

Downstairs again, they almost at once decided to make the huge kitchen into the new tearoom, leaving the area near the Aga as the preparation and cooking area, and having the far end of the room as the tea-tables area.

"We could have six tables for four people each and two small two-people tables, one in the corner and one by the door. We've got enough chairs, or nearly if we use the big window seats with two people on each." Howard walked round seeing it all in his mind's eye.

"Yes and this very big table could go tight against the wall, have a big damask cloth on and be used to put cakes under see-through covers and scones as well. And jams and honey for customers to choose. We could also have a big vase of flowers at the back and make it really inviting and pretty. I'll get Gorse to run me up some tablecloths on her machine, green cotton would be nice." Ling was full of enthusiasm.

"I think we can tackle most of it ourselves, but I think the sink unit should go in the first pantry, and make that the washing up department from now on. In here we shall want a dresser or something to hold all the china for the tearoom."

"Well the dresser in the second pantry is huge. It's a bit shabby but if the builder moved it in here by the Aga, we could paint it white, and it would hold everything. The green 'Beryl' china is what I want. It would look lovely on the dresser, and the cutlery and cruets could go in the cupboards and drawers. Table cloths and napkins in the big long drawer. I think it would make it all very easy to run with everything close at hand and it would look inviting and professional." Ling was smiling delightedly in her excitement. They talked far into the night, making plans for house and garden, Farm Shop and Tearoom. It was a new beginning for Manor Farm, as it was for Howard and Ling and their children.

STRAWBERRIES AND CREAM

Chapter 9

New Beginnings

Chapter 9

New Beginnings

During those weeks of Springtime there were some lovely sunlit days, and in the midst of the bird-song and the bursting open of flowers and leaves, Mary found herself healing in mind and body. When Angel came out of hospital, her family took her straight home to Leicestershire. After a while to get back on her feet again, Angel accepted Mary's invitation to stay for a few weeks at Hill Farm so that she and Peter could be near each other. Mary made the spare room pretty and lovely for her coming. Her arm was still in plaster but her cut face had healed entirely leaving only two tiny scars. Mary's own face had only one scar, which had formed a tiny dimple in her cheek which John assured her was really rather becoming. For both women all the scars both physical and mental were fading from mind and body.

Mary's chickens had come and were growing fast. She had taken charge of all the poultry work once more. Angel was soon helping all she could round the house and outdoors. She and Peter were spending every moment of free time together and their happiness pervaded the whole household. One morning over breakfast John asked the two young ones when they hoped to get married.

"Well," Peter said, after glancing briefly at Angel, "I know we said after the accident that we'd be married as soon as maybe. But we've thought about it and we've decided to wait until mid-Summer. It will give Angel's arm time to finish healing, me the chance to put by a bit more money, and give us both some more courting days and a chance to get a home together." Peter stopped speaking, his eyes on Angel. Mary seeing the expression in them, felt tears blind her eyes and a lump rise in her throat.

She found herself unable to speak. John looked across at her. He knew his Mary so well. He knew he would have to speak for her.

"The reason I asked you when the wedding might be, is because we have been waiting to hear, because we wondered if you would like to live at Bunny Warren? It is a happy little place. Howard and Ling were very happy there. It needs another nice young couple. We thought you might have even asked for the chance to live there by now." He paused for Peter to speak again, but it was Angel who answered,

"We did, we did wonder, but I told Peter that it was a dreadful cheek to ask. I said we ought to wait in case you wanted it for someone else. Oh Aunt Mary, we would love it so, it would make everything perfect." Angel's whole face lit up, her mouth widening into a huge happy smile.

"That's settled then," John was enjoying their obvious pleasure.

"We must pay you rent in the proper way," said Angel shyly.

"Oh no, Peter is a farm worker, he is entitled to a farm worker's cottage. Of course we would never turn you out, if Peter changed his job I mean. Then and only then you could think about paying rent. We shall love you two being there and I'm sure Howard and Ling will be pleased too. Ling has kept on looking after the garden."

"Does having a home make you feel you would speed up the wedding?"

"No, no I don't think so, but we could have a lovely time getting the cottage ready."

"Well all our lads are married, and our attics still not quite empty." John's blue eyes were full of laughter now, "I suggest you have the key to the cottage, which hangs on our dairy wall, just where Howard hung it on the day they moved. Then you can raid our attics and start to furnish your first home."

"What a stunning breakfast time surprise for us. I can hardly believe it." Peter didn't know how to thank them.

"Nonsense you've brought happiness to us older folk, so let us give you back in coin." Mary patted Angel's hand as she got up to clear the table.

Over at Manor Farm work was going ahead at a good pace. Planning had been given for all the work. Kitty had been over several times and Ling spent a lot of time watching the Farm Shop coming into being. The stable walls had been rendered and were being plastered. A new tiled floor had been laid and a false ceiling fitted. Water to a small sink had been laid on and a long formica-topped counter and display shelves had been built. Kitty had brought two dozen baskets for fruit and vegetables and Mary had sent a set of shelves, now painted in white, to use for displaying jams, honey and lemon curd.

None of the farm people kept bees but the other Church Warden, an old friend of Johns had twenty hives in his orchard near the Church. Mr. Partnel had been delighted to be asked to supply honey for the new shop and said they could also have honey on the comb and beeswax when it was in season. In the house at Manor Farm the family were settling in, and Ling and Howard were well on with the preparations for the Tearoom. The builder had moved the sink unit into the first pantry and the dresser out of the second pantry into the main kitchen. Howard and Ling had spent every spare moment painting the dresser and making good the old dresser and sink unit sites. Re-painting the pantry which had been turned into a washing-up room.

They had made a trip into Birmingham and bought two big washing baskets full of green 'Beryl' china from Birmingham Market. Cutlery had come from the local ironmonger in Banworth. The Aga People had provided two large kettles and two heavy duty frying pans for ham and egg teas. The local Market stall had sold them two metal 'Barge' style teapots which were Ling's pride and joy. She felt that tea customers would really enjoy a cuppa out of those. But there were also matching green Beryl teapots for 'pot of tea' customers.

Farm work never ends and Springtime is as busy as any other. Howard, John, Peter and Bill were on the go for longer hours as the evenings grew lighter. At Hill Farm all the cattle which had been penned all Winter were turned out to pasture. Mary always liked to see the young things go out. They had been confined within walls all Winter long. Being released into fields of sweet green meadow grass in the warm Spring sunshine always went to their heads. They would kick up their heels and race about in absolute joy and freedom. It was always one of the best sights in the farming year. Some of the young things went up on the hill, some down to Manor Farm. Once the pens were empty Howard and Billy faced some busy days cleaning the muck out of them with tractors and front end fork lifts. Some of the muck went straight onto spreaders and out to empty fields, most went into a long muck barrow in the back field, ready for spreading in the Autumn when the fields were empty, after harvest and haytime were long past.

Howard also spent time getting used to the new Mayfield garden tractor. It was a neat little machine. Using hoe blades fixed on the tool bar provided, he was able to run up and down each run of strawberries keeping them almost weed-free. The plants were full of flower buds. The next task was to straw them. That is to lay straw on the soil up close round each plant to keep the ripening fruit dry and fresh. The strawing was done one Saturday. Ling and Howard, both children, Peter, Jim and young Bill all met up in the field. Howard brought the Ford Dexta with a small load of dry straw bales from under the barn. The sun shone. Sally Anne sat crowing with joy in the warm Spring day in her pushchair. Young Richard raced up and down, and jumped up on the bales enjoying every moment. Howard dropped off a bale at the top end of each strawberry run. Peter cut the bale strings with his pocket knife. Everyone bent to the task of nesting the straw round the plants. With so many hands for the task, it got done in record time. Angel, her arm still in a loose sling, made tea in the kitchen and brought one of the big barge teapots out. Richard went to help with the gate and carried a basket full of mugs.

"I helped Angel Mummy. Look I carried the basket and I never braked anything," he was bursting with pride.

Kitty, Ling and Mary were busy stocking up the Farm Shop. A few sacks of potatoes had been taken down from Hill Farm. Kitty had brought carrots and bunches of dried herbs. She also had plenty of flowers. In her big garden, lettuces, spring onions, broad beans and early peas would be coming to the shop, as they came ready for gathering along with chives and a selection of salad crops. They had bought and installed a fridge to keep Mary's farm butter and cream. Mary had also filled the jam cupboard with raspberry, strawberry, blackcurrant, marmalade and crab-apple jelly. She had robbed her jam cupboard, but all the farm women planned to make jam especially for the shop next year. Mary had one shelf empty, ready for lemon curd, which had to be made fresh at the last moment.

Lemons and bananas were to be bought in wholesale, from Birmingham fruit market, because Kitty felt that there was bound to be a demand for them. This also applied to tomatoes until Kitty's plants in her biggest greenhouse began to ripen. Twenty four jars of honey had come from John's fellow Church Warden. Also some beeswax. Gorse had sent over three boxes of keeping cooking apples from down in her cellar, and would supply an egg-box full of brown eggs on the day, Mary would supply white eggs to be sold slightly cheaper.

The shop began to look colourful and inviting. The womenfolk were all full of ideas for new items to market in the shop. Howard took the Mayfield tractor up to Hill Farm on the trailer. He cultivated the whole kitchen garden with the scuffle tines. Going through it twice in under two hours. Mary and John sat on the garden seat and watched in amazement to see so much rich brown soil turned and ready for planting in such a short time. They remembered all the years it had had to be done by hand, taking days. They sat and planned what they would plant, with one eye on the Farm Shop sales.

At home at Manor Farm Ling's tearoom was almost ready.

They had bought in the local saleroom six plain square tables and two smaller one.

The big kitchen table had been placed against the wall towards the working, Aga end of the kitchen. The small tables with chairs set round, green cloths looking fresh and cheerful, vases for each table at the ready to be filled with flowers.

Ling was at the washing-up room window one morning when Bill came up the yard on his newly acquired motorbike. Daisy was riding pillion. Howard came out of the pens and joined them. Ling opened the window and called to them.

"Come in and have a cuppa and see my new tearoom."

"Yes, I was bringing them, I was asking Daisy if she was after a job." Howard smiled at Daisy as he spoke. In the kitchen they all sat down, while Ling made coffee.

"Well if she does want a job, she's come to the right place. I'm going to need someone, partly tearoom and partly shop. My sisters-in-law will both come and give a hand, especially Kitty whose children are older, but first, would you like to come?"

"I'd really love that, I've not had no training mind, but I've always helped our Mum with the washing and the little ones. there was six of us you see." Daisy was a plain girl, quite plump with short straight brown hair, but she had a beautiful country-girls skin and warm brown eyes. Her hands were very clean with stubby fingers, and nails trimmed neat and short. A motherly type, Ling decided. Which was probably what had attracted Bill, who as one of eight children, had never rated very high at home.

"Well we'd love you to come .... we open at Easter, Easter Saturday in fact, we shan't open Easter Sunday, but Bank Holiday Monday and the rest of that week. To see how we go with both Shop and Tearoom. Would you be able to start .... well just before, say Maundy Thursday, to get ready. Mrs. Radford at Hill Farm will be cooking for us, but so shall I and I could do with someone else to help. The men are getting busy on both farms now."

"Surely, I've got me bike to come on. What time would I come?"

"Nine o'clock in the morning would suit me. That OK for you? I think both the Shop and the Tearoom will be open from ten thirty until five when the time comes. I'm hoping to do morning coffee, anyway over Easter and holiday weekends. Normal times we'll see how many customers we get."

"What a lovely room this is. Did it used to be the kitchen then?"

"Yes it was but it opens on the yard and is therefore handy for the Shop. Also we felt we could let people see their ham and egg teas being cooked, and at the same time have every-thing to hand to make it easy for us. Come next door and I'll show you the washing-up area. We have those two trolleys to wheel the dirty plates out and the clean things back in. All the china goes on the dresser. Cutlery, cloths and condiments go in the drawers and cupboards under the dresser." Ling explained it all as they went round.

"Oh I like that rack for tea-towels along the wall by the sink .... is it hot?"

"Yes the plumber put that in, the Aga heats it and it gives us dry tea-towels. Are you and Bill going to get married?" Ling asked with friendly curiosity.

"Yes oh yes we are, but we've got to find a place first. Us don't fancy setting up house in our back, with all the kids on top of us. And Bill's Mam's house is even more packed out. We'm saving up, I do a lot of farmwork or anything I can get that's near home. I never fancied town you see."

"Yes I do see Daisy, and I do hope you'll be really happy here with us." A few minutes later, with a roar from the motorbike's engine, the two youngsters were off along the main road.

––––––––––

Up at Hill Farm John and Mary were sitting in the garden enjoying the sunshine. Only during the last few days had it come warm enough for sitting outside. John was reading the Farmer's

Weekly. Mary was knitting a little cardigan for Sally Anne.

"There's a competition here Lass, quite interesting. Have you seen it?"

"No." Mary glanced over his shoulder. "Why John it's on the Women's page, d'you always read the Women's page?"

"I often read some of it. When it's about gardens or poultry, I like to keep up with the other side you see."

"Don't be such an old tease. What's this competition then? Is there a prize?"

"It's six questions about England during the war years. The prize is a bedroom suite."

"Do we need a bedroom suite? Our boys were all born in that bed upstairs Love. It's good enough for me." Mary turned her knitting and began another row.

"I was thinking more of which bed Peter and Angel's three boys might be born in."

"Oh John how lovely, for them to have at Bunny Warren you mean? What are the questions? Let's see if we know the answers."

"I know the answers to five of them, there's three about dairy farming and two about organic fertilizers. I'm sure about those five but the last one's more difficult."

"Try me." Mary laid down her knitting in her lap.

"Say who or what were the 'Industrial Ten'? What kind of a question is that? I think they've purposely put in one hard one that nobody will know."

"That's easy, I know that one. The Industrial Ten were the ten clothing coupons that people got extra if people worked in dirty jobs in factories in the war. My sister used to get them when she worked in a springs factory in West Bromwich."

"My clever Mary, so we know the answers to all six."

"Shall we put it in the post and hope for the best?"

"One snag Lass, there's a sentence to think up."

"What's that?" Mary began another row of knitting.

"Write a sentence of not more than ten words, saying what in your opinion is a farmer's greatest asset."

"Well I would have said his land, if it's good, he'll do well, if it's not he'll fail."

"I think you'll have to leave that one to me Lass. How about a drink of hot tea before I go and call the cows in?" John smiled to himself as he watched Mary's ample bulk walk away across the lawn.

STRAWBERRIES AND CREAM

Chapter 10

Nest Building

STRAWBERRIES AND CREAM

Chapter 10

Nest Building

Peter and Angel were spending most of their time getting their home ready. Up in the farm attic they found, two elderly armchairs for Bunny Warren kitchen, a pine table, two kitchen chairs and a chest of drawers. Not much but it was a start. Gorse offered to make new covers for the armchairs, and curtains to match the kitchen, if Angel would get some material. They managed to find twelve yards in two separate strips in the remnant box on a stall in Banworth Market. It was a creamy linen with a poppy design printed on, which would look cheerful in the kitchen. Gorse as usual made a very good job. She came over bringing her machine. It was easier to cut the material straight onto the chairs in the kitchen at the cottage. She managed to get two cushions out of the material, and Mary found an old feather pillow from which Angel filled two new cushion ticks. Peter and Angel borrowed Howard's van most Saturday afternoons for a couple of hours and he took Angel to several of the local markets. Off the stalls, with only a few pounds to spend they bought bits and pieces of crockery, kitchen utensils, rugs, two clocks and some garden tools and an oak framed mirror. On Sundays they would take a picnic and go down to the cottage laden with their newest purchases. Kitty found them a rather worn carpet for the sitting room. Nothing was new but it was all bought or given with love and gradually Bunny Warren was turning back into a home. Another search of the attic found a small settee.

As Easter drew nearer, Mary began to plan her flowers for decorating the Church for that festival. At the bottom of her garden under the silver birches which Kitty had planted for them in the year of her marriage to Jim; Mary had planted several large clumps of early white narcissus. This year the buds had formed early, each plant holding a dozen or more fat buds. Mary picked two dozen of them and put them in the dairy in a bucket of cold water. With a week to go she felt they would have a very good chance of opening in time. Down the lane, there were plenty of pussy willows, which were less likely than catkins to shed pollen. Kitty had promised white daffodils and cream variegated ivy from her own garden. Mary felt that she would be able to make the pulpit at Church look really pretty. Ling always went with her to decorate the big window by the pulpit. Mary hoped she would have time this year with so much on hand preparing the tearoom. After some discussion John agreed to take Ling and the children down to Church at seven a.m. on Saturday morning, so that she could get her window done and be back in plenty of time for the opening of the Tearoom and Farm Shop. John would take Mary down later in the morning at her usual time.

Meanwhile all the farm women were up to their necks in baking for both Tearoom and Shop. It was their first ever experience of having to work on Good Friday, but it would have to be done. Mary made small one pound weight fruit cakes with plenty of cherries for selling in the shop. To the same recipe she made very large slab cakes for cutting up and serving in the tearoom. She also tackled big batches of shortbread. She felt that the more things that would keep well, that she made beforehand, the easier it would be to tackle the twelve dozen scones she had promised Ling for Easter Saturday. These would have to be made on Good Friday so that they would be really fresh.

Gorse was just as busy at River Farm, but her two 'specials' were easier. She had promised chocolate caramel slices and Bara Brith both for Shop and Tearoom. She spent a couple of hours each morning during the week before Easter getting good stocks of both her products well in hand. Charles was getting boxes of brown eggs ready so that all could be delivered to Ling in good time.

Kitty had a lovely crop of salad stuff ready from her greenhouses. Jim had persuaded a friend at work to ask his

Father, who was a sign-writer, to do two signs for the main road, for which permission had been obtained. The signs were to be green, and were to advertise both Tearoom and Farm Shop in white lettering. Howard had decided that the signs should not go out until Easter Saturday morning. John and Mary, and indeed all the family, wanted to keep the Easter weekend as the very special Christian Festival it had always been. Most especially they wanted to keep Good Friday as a quiet and holy day. If the signs went out on Saturday morning, they felt they would awaken quite enough interest in both Shop and Tearoom, for Easter Saturday, Easter Monday and Easter Week.

When Easter Saturday came, Mary arrived home after decorating the pulpit feeling that her rush was over. The Church had looked beautiful. Her own and Ling's flowers as lovely as anyone's. The scent of the flowers in the Church was repeated in the Churchyard where a carpet of primroses, patches of white violets and thousands of daffodils were out in force to welcome the gentle warmth of Spring sunshine. Coming home beside John in the car the birds had been singing all along the lane. They were still singing in the garden when they took out a tray of tea to the garden seat.

"I hope you haven't overdone it my girl. All that cooking I mean."

"No I enjoyed it. It'll be nice to have the money. Scones have always been easy for me. The only thing I didn't want was to spoil our Easter. You know, yours and mine. Our quiet Easter day has always been so lovely. But I knew it would be all right as soon as Howard came and collected all those scones in the van and they were gone off our pantry shelves, I knew my part was over. I wiped the shelves down and that was it. I'm going to enjoy being just back-up staff in this venture. I don't envy Ling and Howard, in the middle of the action so to speak."

"They're young my Lass, they're the new generation. They'll enjoy the challenge, just like we did when we were young."

"What about Kitty do you think she'll stand up to running the Shop?"

"Kitty's always been a business woman, look how she runs her garden, and Ling will get help if they need it, she's already got Daisy. Now there's a worker, she'll help them and not mind what she does. Never minded getting her hands dirty, Daisy hasn't, just like her Mum that one."

"What do you know about her Mum? That's what I'd like to know." Mary's eyes sparkled.

"I sat next to her in school that's what. When I was in shorts with a patch on the seat and she was in a little white pinny. She had a mole on her leg, inside her knee. I used to reach over, to borrow her rubber I told her, but really it was to get a peek at her mole. In the end she sussed me out and clocked me one in the chops." John's face had remained perfectly serious throughout this confessional. Mary burst out laughing.

"Here, have another cup of tea, you're an old fool John Radford, but I do love you even when you're so soft."

Saturday morning saw the signs go up on the main road for Manor Farm's new business venture. Ling's big side table in the tearoom had two vases full of daffodils and forsythia. Each small table had it's own posy. The big table was filled with chocolate sponges, jam sponges, fruit slab cakes, shortbreads, chocolate slices and tea-breads. All had attractive, domed, see-through covers over them. It made a mouth-watering selection. Cups were set out. The Aga was shining clean. Fresh tea-towels decked the heated towel rail in the washing-up room. All was in readiness.

Outside, the Farm Shop doors were wide open. Baskets of potatoes, vegetables and salad stuff were displayed. Buckets full of daffodils stood outside. Inside Kitty had every shelf stocked. Baskets of eggs, brown and white, nested in straw. Dried herbs hung from the ceiling. Preserves and jars of lemon curd stood in groups on the counter. A glass-topped food display area housed pasties, quiches, savoury pies and sausage rolls. On the lower shelves apple pies displayed crisply brown scalloped edges and leaf designs. Under cellophane wraps, farmhouse fruit cakes, shortbreads and chocolate slices sat in mouth-watering rows. In short everything was ready. Kitty sat calmly in a comfortable chair behind her counter, perfectly confident that customers would come.

In the Tearoom, Ling was in a flutter. Howard was working in the sheds across the yard. She could hear his unconcerned, cheerful whistling. Richard was with him, Sally Anne in her pushchair was also with her Daddy. Daisy was humming a tune as she washed up the last of breakfast pots in the sink. Suddenly Ling heard the sound of voices in the drive, she flew to the window and saw in amazement a large group of women coming in through the yard gate. Once inside, they stood looking round. Ling flew to fling wide the back door.

"Hello, Good Morning," she called.

"Good morning, are you open for coffee and cakes?"

"Oh yes, please do come in."

"Well, we're the Brushstoke W.I., or most of it, we thought we'd give you a good send-off." This was a large cheery looking woman in a red coat, who was obviously in charge.

"I'm Mrs. Barrowcliff, this is the Secretary, Judy Johnson, and this is my Treasurer Pamela Evans. You'll get to know us all in time. We're a friendly lot. Is that the Farm Shop, in the old stable? What a splendid idea. I learned to ride a horse from that stable. Lovely mare she was, called Melody I recall. Tell you what. I'll count us up and then you can make the coffee while we have a quick shifty round the Farm Shop." She turned away and counted up her retinue with a quick pointing finger.

"I think we're twenty-eight, give or take a few. So that's twenty-eight cups of coffee and some plates of cakes for everyone. Now ladies, let's go and look in the shop."

"Ling and Daisy set to work at a run. Two kettles and a pan of milk went on the Aga. Cakes were set on plates for all eight tables. Cups and saucers were massed at the ready. Ling turned shining eyes to Daisy.

"I think you'd better go and help Kitty serve all that throng in the shop. They'll probably get back in here in ones and twos and I can manage that."

Daisy ran down the yard into the jam-packed shop. Howard had heard the commotion and was behind the counter with Kitty weighing out potatoes, and filling egg boxes. Daisy was soon serving two women with lettuces and pots of jam. Afterwards Kitty likened it to a swarm of locusts. As Ling had predicted the women progressed quite slowly to the Tearoom. Most of them carrying a bag full of produce. All seemed to like the big airy tearoom area and being able to actually watch their coffee being made. The room rapidly filled up, it was rather like serving a flock of chattering starlings. Everyone was talking their heads off and while they talked, cups of coffee were drunk and refilled. Cakes and pastries were vanishing before Ling's wide-eyed joy and amazement. The neat card menus were read and re-read against future visits. When at last the red-coated lady rose to go, they all rose, almost as one. Ling was strongly reminded of flocks of wild geese flying South for the Winter. They queued up to pay their bills and they were gone as quickly as they had come, leaving the tearoom as though a herd of buffalo had passed through.

Ling sank into a chair laughing and crying at the same time.

"Well, what a right howd'youdo that was," said Daisy matter of factly, as she began to stack dirty crockery on a trolly. Howard's head came round the door.

"My God Kitty, it's just as bad in here, if not worse, come and look. Are you there wife? Don't just sit there. Don't you reckon we all deserve a cup of coffee?" He glanced round at the general muddle, "that's if there's any clean cups left."

150

Easter Sunday was a quiet day as Mary had hoped. Howard and Ling joined Mary and John for the eleven o'clock service, and for the first time Peter and Angel came as well. Young Richard and Sally Anne made up the party. Howard was in charge of Sally Anne and did his best to keep her quiet. No one minded the occasional squeak anyway. They occupied two pews and the rest of the Church was thronged with old friends and neighbours. The scent all round of flowers was almost over-powering. John stood the Church door half open because it was so warm. The first time during the many years he had been Church Warden, that he could remember having the door left open at Easter time. The wonderful old Easter hymns could be heard across the churchyard and through the cottage window to old Miss Dunn, who lay bedridden in her daughter's back parlour. They gave her great pleasure.

All the family had dinner at Hill Farm. Mary had left a good roast in the oven, and a boiled fruit pudding steaming on the top. Most of the talk centred on the Shop and Tearoom, and yesterday's successes. Ling and Kitty had been most surprised that so many of the people who had come had been local. After the W.I. rush in the morning, Ling had cooked Ham and Egg lunches for three workmen who were painting a nearby house. During the afternoon several passing cars came in for tea. Most people went for a look round the shop. Most bought something, honey, jam, lemon curd and pastry items had brought the most sales on the Saturday afternoon. Kitty and Ling were both excited by the response that their new venture had received. On their very first day they had won the support of the local village folk. Ling felt that nothing could have pleased her more, or given her so much hope for the future.

On Easter Monday Ling and Howard were grateful to wake up to sunshine yet again. As they had hoped it brought them a

151

steady flow of customers for both Shop and Tearoom. They sold out of sponge type cakes by lunch-time in the Shop and Ling served a couple of dozen people with coffee. Most of them were off the road. People who were out for the day, coaxed out for a run in the car in the sunshine. One lady summed it up to Ling in the Tearoom.

"We felt we couldn't waste the Easter sunshine, so often it's wet or showery at Easter."

One fact was definitely being proved. People came off the road seeking refreshment, tea or coffee, but once they were off the road they all wanted to see inside the Shop. Once in the Shop they all bought something.

Kitty had brought her two boys, Simon and Nicky and they both enjoyed playing on the bales in the stackyard and helping their Mum in the Shop. Kitty found that she was selling on all fronts. Cakes were especially popular. People out for the day, thinking to take something homemade home from the country to make a quick easy tea come supper on arrival back home. Once again jams, preserves, honey and lemon curd were selling well, as they had done on Easter Saturday. One family bought a whole sackful of potatoes to take home to Birmingham.

In the Tearoom Ling and Daisy were kept busy. Several families out for the day ordered ham and egg teas. All the customers seemed to enjoy very much the fact that they could watch their meal being cooked in the big Aga pans. Everyone was given the choice of one or two eggs. Everyone could hear and smell the delicious slices of ham frying in the pan. A large plate of brown and white bread and butter was served with ham and egg teas. Also the pot of tea was included in the price. One man coming to pay his Bill congratulated Ling saying,

"That was a grand tea you served us, I can see you're going to be popular. I think we could easily make a run out this way in the car, and a ham and egg tea with you folks, a regular feature. Anyway Love congratulations and thanks for a really good tea." He put a handsome tip on the counter by the till and left, all smiles.

Mary's scones had sold really well on Bank Holiday Monday. With strawberry jam and thick whipped cream from Hill Farm's Jerseys, a lot of customers had chosen cream teas.

By five thirty the Tearoom was empty. Kitty came in having shut the Shop.

"Any chance of a nice hot cup of tea and one of Mary's scones, before I take these tired boys home to their Dad?"

"I'll make a fresh pot," Daisy came in from the washing-up room, rolling down her sleeves. Ling was clearing tables onto the trolley and seeing off the last couple from the twosome by the window.

"Let's all have a cuppa together, it's time to close now anyway." A few minutes later Howard, who was not milking that night, came in and joined them. Nicky and Simon ran in from the yard and were each given a buttered scone. They at once ran out again.

"How children love a farm, my two have been as happy as sandboys all day round the yards here. It's been a good day for us all hasn't it? Good weekend, come to that." Kitty pushed her hair back from her forehead and stretched her legs out under the table.

"This tea tastes wonderful."

"Yes after all the talk and being run off our feet. To sit and drink a cup of tea is just like heaven. But don't think I'm moaning. I can't believe how well we've done. Only thing is Howard's just putting Mum's last scone in his mouth. We're going to need a lot more of a lot of things, if we're going to keep open all the week."

"I think we should, we shan't do as well as these last two days but as it's Easter Week I think we'll get quite a bit of trade and people will get to know we are here." And so it was decided to open daily from ten until five for the whole of Easter week. After that they would open weekends only until Whitsun, when they would again open for the whole week. When the tea was drunk Ling stood up.

"Now you two, Kitty and Daisy, get off home. Howard and I

will finish clearing up. I'll ring Mum about scones for morning if she makes a couple of dozen, that should do us. I'll make sponges first thing in the morning. Gorse knows we need more caramel slices. Charles is bringing them, and brown eggs tomorrow morning." Ling began to wheel the last of the crocks out to the sink.

"I'll bring some salad stuff tomorrow for the shop." Kitty moved towards the door.

"The cash and the slips are in the brown bag in the dresser drawer. You keep them here Ling. Jim'll come when you say; bank it all up and write up the books; pay us all out for goods supplied. Anyway just let him know. Goodnight to you all, see you in the morning." A few minutes later they heard her car drive out of the yard. Daisy had put her jacket on, and ridden off on her bicycle with a cheerful wave.

"I'll do the crocks, you set up the tables and see to the food table." Howard was cheerful and full of energy. Ling buckled to and set to work in spite of aching feet, and began to prepare the tearoom for the next day. Clean cloths where necessary and all food on the big table put away in tins on the shelves. Everywhere wiped down and clean, and every now and again a quick peep into the office, to see how Sally Anne and Richard were doing. In fact Richard was playing quietly with his fort and soldiers. Sally Anne was sitting in her little reclining chair wriggling her toes on the rattle toys which hung along the bottom rail.

"Oh you are good little souls aren't you, Mummy's nearly finished, then we'll all have our tea." Soon they were turning out the outside light, locking the back door, closing the sitting room curtains and settling in front of the sitting room fire with a tray of tea that was just for themselves. A happy little family in their new home.

———————

While Easter weekend advanced in the tearoom and farm

shop, up at Hill Farm John and Mary were enjoying the warm spell of Spring weather. All Mary's poultry were out on grass. Egg production was going down a little. The hens were going out of lay and the pullets were coming into lovely condition and would be laying by the end of April. John got out the tractor and moved all the hen pens onto fresh grass. Mary's chicks, now losing all their fluffy look and coming into feather were moved into a strip of grassy ground behind the workshop. Howard and Peter made a wire run for them, to keep them confined and form an added protection against foxes.

Peter and Howard lime-washed all the empty calf pens and out-buildings. Later in the week when it became showery all the men, cleared out and tidied the workshop, and then began to check over all the haymaking machinery ready for haytime. Mary loved these quieter times when no main jobs were on the menu. All the men were working round the yards near home, meals were therefore on time. Mid-morning drinks were served in the kitchen. No flasks had to be carried across the fields to thirsty workers. Angel had returned home to Leicestershire, and now that her arm was mobile she was again working in Kitty's nursery garden. Her Father had wanted to get her another car, but both Angel and Peter felt that they would rather wait until just before the wedding and then buy a shared vehicle. Angel's Father had suggested helping with the cost as a wedding present, which they had both been very pleased to accept. Now that Howard had his own van, the Farm car was often free for Peter to borrow, to drive over to take Angel out at weekends and in the evenings.

Mary made scones and other goodies for the tearoom and farm shop as they were needed. Jim kept the accounts for both the new ventures, and saw to it that neat little payment envelopes went to Mary, Gorse and Kitty for their goods and also to Ling for all her cooked items, as this was the easiest way to keep the books straight. All four women enjoyed the cooking and getting their pay packets. Mary was setting hers aside to buy Angel and Peter a lovely wedding present. John was biding his time over the wedding present until he saw if his efforts in that direction bore fruit.

On the first fine Sunday after Easter, Mary was sitting in the garden after dinner. They had been on their own for dinner and were enjoying a quiet day. John came out of the front door and across the lawn, puffing his pipe and looking hugely pleased with himself. In his hand he held an envelope.

"I've been waiting to show you this on our own. With Pete having gone in the car over to Angel's, I thought it would be a good time."

"When did that come?" Mary smiled up at him from her knitting which had been lying in her lap, while she dozed in the sunshine.

"On Friday actually, I've been biding my time, till we could be alone. Here you read it for yourself." He handed her the long white envelope,

"It's got the Farmer's Weekly address printed on the back, what are they writing to you for? Oh John. That competition! You sent it in .... you won!"

"Have a look you softy." Mary took the single sheet out of the envelope and scanned it's contents. Her eyebrows flew up.

"John, you won, how clever of you, they want you to go and choose a bedroom suite. Well I'm coming to help if that's the case. Do we have to go to London?"

"No, read it again Lass, Birmingham or Coventry is our nearest. Farmer's Weekly want us to phone and make arrangements. Lewis's Birmingham is one of the stores mentioned or Owen Owens Coventry. Which d'you think would be best?"

"Well I think Owen Owens, they have lovely things in their furniture department."

"All right, Owen Owens it is. I'll ring the Farmer's Weekly first thing in the morning and see when their blokes can meet us there. Have to make some excuse, keep it secret from Peter. He'll be about on Monday again."

"Well you can phone when he's across the yard, and we can

156

just say we're going shopping when we go to Coventry to choose. I shall enjoy that, we can have tea at that nice tea place in Hertford St. The wool shop's next door, I can pop in and get some yellow wool, for a cardigan for Kitty. I promised I'd make her one. Fancy you and me going out to tea, like we used to years ago." Mary picked up her knitting again with a most satisfied expression on her face.

The rest of the day passed peacefully by, and it was not until they were in bed and just dropping off to sleep that Mary remembered something.

"John?" she said sleepily.

"Um .... what is it Lass?"

"That sentence, in the competition about a Farmer's Best Asset in ten words?"

"Yes, what about it?"

"Did you put what I said? Really that his land was his greatest asset?"

"No Love I'm afraid I didn't."

"What did you put instead?"

"I just put, 'For this farmer, my wife Mary is my greatest asset.'"

"Oh John, did you really? Did you mean it?"

"Of course, you know that, now let's get to sleep, we've got to be up early don't forget."

"John, you're a most lovely man. Goodnight Dear." Mary leant over and planted a kiss on his cheek, then she sank down into her pillows and fell sound asleep.

———————

After Easter was over Manor Farm settled into a steady routine. Both shop and tearoom were opened at weekends only. They were quite busy on both Saturday and Sunday afternoons. After the first two weeks, they did not open until two p.m. on Sundays. Howard and Ling found this much nicer. They could get to Church with the children on Sunday mornings as they had always done, with John and Mary. The shop was doing well all day on Saturdays. They had been surprised at how many local people came to both shop and tearoom. Ling had tactfully found out what the Post Office in Brushstoke sold before they had opened. She had not wanted to set up in direct competition, so had not stocked sweets or groceries. Fortunately the Post Office didn't sell any fruit or vegetables or any kind of garden produce. In fact they did not sell eggs either or dairy products, and no home made foods.

Soon Kitty had a lot of regular customers from the village coming in to buy eggs and often taking a lettuce or vegetables. Home made savouries were also popular and they were soon taking orders for quiches and Ling's Steak and Kidney pies. Kitty ran the shop almost single-handed. She would bring Nicky and Simon with her, and a car load of vegetables and flowers. They still employed Daisy for a lot of hours. She cleaned the shop and filled up the shelves, turning her hand to any job that needed doing. She worked alongside Ling in the tearoom. Fine weekends saw a lot of people coming to the tearoom. Morning coffee on Saturday attracted local women and their friends. Saturday afternoons saw people off the road for ham and eggs as a lunch which often ran over well into the afternoon. Sunday afternoons were for cream tea people. The finer the weather, the more would come. Only opening at the weekends helped Ling to arrange her life into compartments. She had time for her garden, and to help on the farm, which she had always loved. She helped Howard with the sheep and did some tractor work. Harrowing, rolling, all the lighter field tasks, which she felt kept her hand in. She was finding what a treasure Daisy was. Daisy now helped her twice during the week. One day with bedrooms, and one with downstairs cleaning and minding the children in the afternoon. This was Ling's precious afternoon off. Then she was free as the air, often she walked across the fields and under the railway tunnel and up the Hill Farm front fields to Mary. They would garden, or talk, or sit in the sunshine. Sometimes she would take the van and drive over to see Kitty or Gorse. Sometimes she and Howard would go to a farm sale or market. Daisy loved to be left in charge of the children. She played games with them, just as she did at home with her own little brothers and sisters. All the family especially John and Mary, found great joy in seeing Howard and Ling growing into the new life they were building together and yet still as John put it,

"Finding time for us old folks."

———————————————

STRAWBERRIES AND CREAM

Chapter 11

Haytime

STRAWBERRIES AND CREAM

Chapter 11

Haytime

The warm sun and the heavy showers in late April and early May brought a lush growth to the pastures all round both farms. Seed heads began to form on the grasses in the hay field and patches of white clover amongst the grass, came into bloom. Bees hung on the flower heads sucking out the nectar and hopefully some of the bounty was carried to the hives by the Churchyard wall which supplied the honey for the Farm Shop.

In the workshop at Hill Farm , Peter, Howard and John finished checking over and greasing the three mowers. The turners and two balers stood ready, oiled, greased and fitted with new parts where needed. The first field to be ready for mowing was a Hill Farm field close beside the beech woods near Bunny Warren. Howard and Peter went, tractors roaring, with a mower each. Peter was facing his first haytime at the farm and John felt that Howard would show Peter the ropes if they started into the mowing together. When they were well started, Howard felt his usual enthusiasm for making and bringing in the hay harvest. The very smell of the fresh mown grass was a pleasure to him. Peter on the other tractor was in a different kind of cloud cuckoo land altogether. Angel had come back to give them a hand with the hay harvest. She was to stay for two weeks at least. Peter found himself more head over heels in love than ever. Kitty had brought her over in the car that very morning. The sight of her wide smile and cheeky tip-tilted lightly freckled nose and most of all her wildly curling mane of hair, set off so well by her green work shirt and old brown slacks, had made his heart leap in his chest. He had not seen her for nearly a week. It had seemed like a lifetime to Peter. Now here she was, so happy and so at ease.

He had almost leapt up from the table and flung his arms about her and kissed her again and again. He had instead grinned at her and simply said,

"Hi there, how's tricks?" But she had known, known exactly how he was feeling, and all she had done was fling him a backward glance and go tripping upstairs to unpack her bag. Well he'd catch her later and show her who was boss. As the tractors droned round and round the field following on after each other, Peter's thoughts never left Angel's loveliness for very long. When she came into the field with bottles of tea for them, half way through the morning, her eyes teased him, when the two men, tractors silent, stood drinking their tea under the shadow of the beechwood. Howard, sensing the tension between them, felt very much in the way, but covered it by chatting about the crop.

"Make a few bales this will this time. Heaviest crop I ever remember in May," he said turning a heavy swath with the toe of his boot.

"So we'll be romping in the hay if this dries out well." Peter looked at Angel as he spoke.

"Yes, Ling's hoping we can have strawberries and cream in the hay. She's got quite a few beginning to turn red." Howard smiled and passed Angel his empty tea bottle, and strode back across the cut swaths to his tractor. While his back was turned Peter swooped on Angel and kissed her mouth lingeringly. She struggled wildly to free herself.

"Let me go Peter, he'll see us. Let me go."

"My dear girl I haven't kissed you for a week, I'm starved, it's time we got married, just through the trees, there's our little house to be, and here I am not allowed to kiss you in case Howard sees us. Anyway he's keeping his back turned, he knows the score well enough." Peter let her go however and shortly afterwards went back to work. Angel carried the basket of empty bottles back up the lane to Hill Farm. In the kitchen Mary was well on with the dinner. When she came in the door Mary smiled at Angel, noticing at once her rosy cheeks and slightly tumbled appearance. Young Love, she thought to herself, out loud she just asked a very normal question.

"How are they getting on with the field? Dinner will be ready in half an hour or so. Will they be done in time?"

"Oh yes, Howard said about half an hour to finish and it's taken me over fifteen minutes to walk back. Can I help with anything?"

"Well if you could lay the table for me Dear, then we shall be ready when they get here. And I was wondering if you could do them a drink in the middle of the afternoon. They'll be nearer home this afternoon. They're mowing this back field after dinner. And could you give the hens two buckets of corn about half past three. John and I are hoping to pop into Coventry for a bit of shopping. Only if we go now there's no hay at risk, like it will be in a weeks time."

"I shall love to mind everything while you're gone, shall I collect the eggs and what about the little chicks?"

"Oh you're a help, it would be nice to get back to not much work. The eggs could do with collecting about four, and the chicks water will want filling up. Anytime you're free will do for that, and their feed troughs. The chick feed is in my meal pen. First bag on the left. The two buckets of corn for the hens, they have it just scattered on the grass, I've fill the buckets ready in the pen."

"I shall manage fine, it's lovely to be back here, and part of the farm again." Angel blushed slightly.

"We've all missed you Lass, especially Peter you know. He does love you so my Dear. I shouldn't leave it too long before you set the wedding date."

"I know, since the car crash I miss him dreadfully when we are not together. I tease him and string him along that I don't care, but really I sometimes feel desperate."

"Don't tease him too much Lass, men are only overgrown little boys you know, they need us to show that we love them."

"Who must we show that we love them, me I hope?" John came round the door and seized Mary round the waist, danced her round the kitchen and kissed her soundly on the mouth.

When she managed to escape from his embrace, she gasped for breath and then managed to speak.

"Nothing to do with you John Radford. Women's talk and anyway listeners never hear any good of themselves. Get you washed, dinner's nearly on the table. Can you hear the tractors coming Lass? Have a listen on the yard." Angel ran outside and sure enough she could hear the roar of the tractors coming up the lane.

"They'll be here in a minute Mary, tearing up the lane they are."

"Good, sooner they get here, the sooner John and I can get away, and that means the sooner we'll be back."

John and Mary set off for Coventry at about one o'clock; having changed into tidy clothes and left Angel in charge of the washing up. In this she was ably helped and hindered by Peter, who at once offered to dry the dishes for her. Howard went off to his set of tackle and made a start on mowing the back field. The washing up was interrupted with several lovers exchanges in the kitchen. It was all done and tidy by the time John and Mary came down the stairs ready for Coventry. Peter was back on his tractor. Angel flushed and dishevelled ran off down the orchard to fill the chicks water trough, and she was back in time to give Mary and John a quick wave off down the drive.

After they had gone Angel ran to the back field gate and sat on the top bar to watch the two sets of tackle circling the field. The two men intent upon their work. Howard's dark head bent to his task, went by her first. Then Peter's fair curly head also bent over the steering, but taking time to wave his hand and blow her a kiss as his machine travelled by. Angel thought how happy she was and of the life they planned together. Of the little house waiting through the woods. Then she noticed the light breeze catching the standing grass and waving it like the waves of the sea. How beautiful it all is she thought. The sunlight casting silver patches on the swaths of mown hay, falling in steady rhythm beneath the mower's knife. Occasionally an animal came out of the uncut grass, and ran for shelter. A couple of rabbits at one corner, then a great rust coated hare, with long ears black-tipped as he lolloped across the mown swaths. In the far corner a fox slipped swiftly out of the mowing grass running for the cover of the woodland beyond the lane. Angel could hear wood-pigeons cooing in the oaks near the house and hens cackling in the orchard as they came off the laying nests. She would go and collect the eggs. She fetched the basket from the kitchen and walked down the garden towards the orchard.

———————————

John and Mary left the car in Pool Meadow car park and walked through the town to Owen Owens store. At the main door they waited, looking for the young man Leslie Banks, who was to meet them there at two p.m. At first they couldn't see any young man waiting anywhere near the door.

"John do you think we could've come to the wrong door?"

"Well this is the main door, and it's only just on two o'clock, wait a minute who's this?" At that moment a young woman in a smart grey suit and black court shoes, handbag swinging from her shoulder, fair hair cut and shaped to her head, came straight up to them holding out her hand to Mary.

"How do you do, are you by any chance Mr. and Mrs. John Radford? I'm Leslie Banks from Farmer's Weekly."

"Oh yes, how unexpected, we thought you must be a man. We were looking for a young man Miss Banks." Said Mary shaking hands with Leslie Banks in her usual friendly fashion.

"Congratulations Mrs. Radford on winning our competition." Leslie Banks smiled at them both.

"Oh no, that was our John, Miss Banks, he answered all the questions except one. And he made up the sentence, I had no idea until after he'd won that he hadn't put in the farmer's greatest asset as being his land. When he told me what he had put in I really couldn't believe it."

"We had a lot of entries Mrs. Radford, but only your

husband's sentence appealed to all five judges."

"Were the judges farmers Miss Banks?" asked John.

"Oh yes, one of them was the head of the National Farmer's Union."

"Well if most farmers told the truth, most would choose the wife as the greatest asset. Our farm wouldn't be the happy place it is without my Mary." Said John firmly. Mary flushed scarlet, and Leslie Banks seeing this, at once changed the subject of their conversation.

"Well what about the bedroom suite then? Let's go up and choose it. We can walk round and see what they have available first." They went up in the lift to the furniture department, and found the Manager there waiting for them. Mary felt like Royalty as they were shown a large selection of bedroom suites. Some were very expensive and opulent and John and Mary felt a bit out of their depth. Mary whispered to John,

"These are useless, none of these would fit into Bunny Warren." Mary decided to take the bull by the horns, turning to Miss Banks she said,

"You see Miss Banks, please don't think we are being choosy, it's just that we are giving this suite to our nephew Peter. Peter works on the farm and he's marrying a really lovely girl. They're going to live in our cottage. We really wanted something suitable for a cottage. You know with beams and old oak floors. Something a bit plainer, something cottagey." Mary looked a bit flustered, trying to make them understand. She need not have worried, Owen Owens Manager understood at once.

"Well Mrs. Radford, in that case come this way. Mostly you see we have to cater for houses in the suburbs of Coventry. They're after painted woods and padded head-boards. Nowadays most beds have padded head-boards so there's almost no oak about, but we do have this which you may like." They came to series of curtained off alcoves. Each was furnished with a carefully arranged bedroom suite. In the one the Manager had paused by there was a double divan bed with a quilted head-board covered in tiny pink roses. The bed legs were curved and chubby in dark wood. The dressing table had an oval mirror over a kidney shaped glass top and three drawers either side, the same dark wood as the bed legs. The wardrobe was wide and quite low, hanging cupboards with a small carved oak-leaf motif on each door. In the centre three drawers with a flat polished surface above, and a recessed mirror matching the one on the dressing table.

"This is just right. It is so suitable for a cottage, what do you think John?"

"I think it's ideal, low wardrobe, that'll fit under the low ceilings at Bunny Warren. But is it within the price range of our competition win?"

"Yes, yes it is, and it leaves you with," the manager made a few quick calculations, "£45 in hand."

"Do you want to choose something else as well?" asked Leslie Banks.

"Or could we stick with the bedroom suite which will be lovely and have a forty-five pound gift voucher for our young people to come and choose some things after they are married?" The manager readily agreed and invited them to have a cup of tea in his office. John made their excuses, he had promised Mary tea and cream cakes in Hertford Street. Having arranged to ring up and sort out delivery of the bedroom suite, Mary and John said their goodbyes and thank yous and were soon walking down Hertford Street. It was only a little after three o'clock and the teashop was almost empty. Mary chose a table near the window. She sank into a comfortable chair.

"Oh John, I'm that glad to be on our own again. They were nice folks but talk, talk, talk. I must be a real country bumpkin. D'you know I'm tired out?"

"Oh no you're not, we're just ordinary country folk, town folk live faster somehow. But that Lass meant well, that Miss Leslie Banks, and she had a nice pair of legs on her."

"John trust you to notice that." John ordered tea and cream cakes and they spent a happy half hour eating chocolate eclairs and meringues at the table in the window, watching the shoppers passing to and fro. Then John paid the Bill while Mary popped next door to the wool shop for enough lemon yellow wool for a cardigan and a nice pattern. As the car drew away from the town and they began to pass fields and woodland Mary felt herself relax.

"Home John, what a pleasure. I've enjoyed it all but I'm never sorry to get back to Hill Farm. I wonder how Howard and Peter got on with the back field. And then there's Angel with the poultry. She's a good Lass you know John. She'll make our Peter a good wife, a real country girl like Ling she is."

"I'll give you that she's a very nice girl, but no one's such a special as our Ling you know Love."

"Oh I know John, remember when Ling came, and Howard couldn't keep his eyes off her? So good at all the farm jobs she was and yet such pretty ways with it."

"That's not altered you know Love, our Howard still thinks the world of Ling. They're as much in love as ever."

"I know, it's the joy of my life, especially now they've got their own farm, right close adjoining ours."

"Here we are Lass." John turned in at the farmyard gate, and drew to a halt by the back door. In the house Angel had laid the table with a bowl of flowers at the centre. Bread and butter was cut, fruit cake and sponge, jam and the cheese dish. Egg cups stood by everyones plates. On the Aga the kettle steamed away and beside it the small saucepan of boiling water ready to boil the eggs, a basket of eggs stood ready. Cups and saucers were set out and the teapot stood warming on top of the cooker. Angel came to the door to welcome them home.

"Peter and Howard are sharing a bath, they'll be down in a minute. The field's all cut. I got eighty eggs and they're packed in the eggbox. The chicks are fine. Have you had a nice time?"

"Well Love you have done splendid, what a welcome home. She's a real good girl isn't she John?"

"Yes Lass I reckon we're well in the way of another perfect daughter-in-law, well she is almost isn't she?" Howard and Peter came into the kitchen at that moment.

"Almost your daughter-in-law or almost perfect Uncle John?" Peter was grinning as he spoke.

"Well both really Lad I suppose." John sat down in his chair at the head of the table. Angel was by the Aga.

"How many eggs does everyone want?"

"I should allow two each Dear, those boys will easily put away two each, if you and I can't, Howard can manage an extra one." Mary suggested.

"We're going to be late finishing milking tonight Dad. Young Bill's gone to get the cows in and get a start, I felt we must finish the field and have a bite to eat. I'll get across there as soon as I've eaten."

"And I'll go." Peter reached for bread and butter as he sat down.

"Eggs need another moment or two." Angel began pouring tea into the cups and passing the cups across to Howard and Peter. A few minutes later the family were sitting at table enjoying their boiled eggs.

"You look cheery Peter." John noticed Peter's bright face across the table.

"Well Angel's named the day. We're to be married between haytime and harvest. How long does it take to get the hay in Uncle John?"

"Oh months if there's a lot of rain." Howard interrupted laughing all over his face.

"Depends on the weather Lad, but it takes three weeks to put up the banns, whatever the weather." John said cheerfully. Everyone was still laughing at Howard's earlier remark.

"How lovely, a wedding, we haven't had a wedding since Charles married Gorse. How long ago is it?" Mary's mind went back to that happy time.

"Well the twins are two years old, so it's got to be three years ago I reckon."

"Well this one won't be in our Church will it Lass? You will want to be married in your own village I'm sure." Mary got up to refill the cups as she spoke.

171

"Yes, in a way I'd like it to be here, but Mother and Dad will want it to be in our Church where I was christened. What I did wonder was, do you think Ling would let us have the reception in the Tearoom?" Angel's eyes lit up as she spoke.

"I should think she'd love it." Howard's voice came between mouthfuls of fruit cake.

"It would be nice, and we could all help." Mary brightened at the thought.

"It's only about half an hour from Angel's village Church over to Manor Farm, so it could be managed," Peter stood up as he spoke.

"Anyway we must get milking, and I'm on air now. How many fields can we cut tomorrow Uncle John, the sooner we get em all cut the better!"

During the next few days there were some showers of rain. John was not worried, the glass was rising and the showers would, as he put it, wash the dust out of the hay. They cut another field, this time at Manor Farm. It was ten acres of meadow hay, close to Brushstoke Station. It would be carted to Howard's barns to use as feed for the in-lamb ewes next Winter. At the weekend the sun came out and there was a slight breeze; drying weather. Soon the men were run off their feet turning the hay and cutting two more fields. Howard and Peter spent a day at River Farm mowing Charles' fields. Gorse gave them a good dinner in her farmhouse kitchen. Howard thought how much improved the fields were compared with when Charles had first bought the farm. The twins in their play-pen were in the little yard where a few years back Billy, Charles' eldest boy by his first marriage, had played in the early days when Gorse had first come here as housekeeper. It was a happy mealtime. Howard felt the happiness of this family and saw the absolute contentment in his brother's face.

At the end of the day Charles saw them off along the drive which led over the river bridge to the main road.

―――――――――――

Two days later, they began baling the hay at Hill Farm. Ling came to use the Ford Dexta and row up the hay, all the family were busy. Mary with meals, minding Sally Anne and Richard, and sending out baskets of drinks to the haymakers. Angel helped wherever she could, with meals in the house, with poultry in the orchard, and with getting the cows in and learning to milk under Billy's instruction. At the weekend Jim came to help in the hay, and Kitty to run the Farm Shop single-handed.

Ling, helped enormously by Daisy, who worked like a black, ran the Tearoom, cutting down the opening hours because the hay was more important. Daisy and Ling also picked the few strawberries which were already ripe. There were not enough to open for Pick Your Own, so Mary and Gorse made them into jam. Mary got up at five a.m. one Friday to make some scones. She was used to early mornings so found it no hardship.

The fine weather held and the bales began to be loaded and carted under cover. It was a sight which John was thankful to see. Two young Lads, friends of Bills, came to help with the carting. It left Howard free to mow the rest of the fields and bale hay for several old customers on the contract side. When hay harvest was about half done, and John had fifteen acres to mow at Manor Farm and only a small eight acre field near the house at Hill Farm, the young people began to plan their wedding. A heavy shower during the night gave the haymakers a breathing space.

Peter and Angel took a couple of days off and went to Angel's home to spend time with her parents and put up the banns in the local village church. Angel and her Mother were joined by Kitty in a days shopping in Leicester. They bought her wedding dress and two little dresses for her two small bridesmaids. They also bought cutlery and bedding for Bunny Warren, which was to be Angel's parents gift for the wedding. The wedding date was fixed for July tenth, which was a Saturday. As soon as Peter saw the weather beginning to settle down again he knew that their free time was ending.

"Back to haymaking first thing in the morning Love." He gave Angel a big hug.

"It's been nice to be free of farm-work for two or three days but we can't let Uncle John down, can we?"

"No of course we can't, we understand that but it's been lovely to have you here these few days." Angel's Mother smiled her serene smile, which had very much the look of Angel in it Peter noticed.

"I think we should go back tonight in case the hay's fit tomorrow." Angel looked across the tea table at her Father.

"I'll run you back after tea but we'll call at the Garage and have a look at that little car they've got for sale, I'd like to see you start out with a vehicle of your own of some sort. If you like that one your Mum and I will help with the cash for it."

"Dad you're very good to us considering I smashed up the little Morris."

"That wasn't your fault my girl, anyway this is a Morris as well but not the same model. She's done a few miles but she's a tidy looking little vehicle and you won't want to do umpteen miles, mostly shopping and Peter getting to work on wet days. Is there a garage at the cottage?"

"No but Uncle John's got plenty of timber at the farm. He's thinking of helping me build a garage on the empty bit of land just beyond the cottage which belongs with the house. He thought Howard'd give a hand and we'd get it done in the Winter when work's slack on the farm."

"Well we'll look at the car anyway, if you do have it, it would be nice to get it under cover." They all rose from the table and the two women cleared for washing up.

"You help your Mum do that, then get your traps packed, we need to be at the garage before six." At the garage, Peter and

Angel were both very taken with the four-seater black Morris. It had a scratch or two but it was a nice little car.

"Look Lad I'll buy it for you here and now and you can give me fifty towards it when you can manage it." Angel's Father smiled with enjoyment at their delighted expressions. He took out his cheque-book and rested it on the bonnet of the car, then he turned to the garage man.

"Could they take it away with them now, if I do the insurance on the phone with my N.F.U. man this evening? I see it's taxed for three months."

"Certainly, you being an old customer Sir, I can't see anything against it."

"Have you got your driving licence Peter?"

"Yes here it is, always carry it here in my wallet." Peter was absolutely beaming.

"Well fill it up with petrol and I'll put the cost of the fuel in the cheque. Save me driving them back to Banworth, this will," he winked at Angel as he spoke. It was all done in five minutes. Angel's and Peter's bags were transferred to the Morris and they climbed in, after Angel had given her Dad a kiss and a big hug. They drove off down the road and Angel's Dad turned back to the garage man still standing by the petrol pumps with the cheque in his hand, a slightly dazed smile on his face.

"You're only young once you know Jack. They're going to be married next month you know. Here in our own Church. Her Mum and I are so pleased. He's a nice lad, used to be a mechanic, like you. Now works on his Uncle's farm just outside Banworth. Lovely cottage his Uncle's letting them have for them to live. We wanted them to have the best start we could."

"Nothing like love's young dream is there?" Jack watched the young folk driving away out of sight over the hill.

"Nothing, I often wish I could have my courting days over again."

"Don't we all, don't we all?"

STRAWBERRIES AND CREAM

Chapter 12

Picnic in the Hay

STRAWBERRIES AND CREAM

Chapter 12

Picnic in the Hay

Under the Dutch barn at Hill Farm, three bays of sweet green hay scented the air. The bales stacked high and neat were safe from the weather. Twelve acres of hay were still out. As it was midweek there was no shop or tearoom to worry them. John felt that with a fine day and a full home gang, now was the time to get in the last of the crop. Howard had got to the farm after walking to work across the fields early in the day. Everywhere had been beautiful that early morning. A light mist over the reservoir, the sun just rising beyond the hill. Birds singing and young rabbits grazing on the cinder track by the railway line. The May blossom was just coming into flower, buttercups shone on the banks and across the front fields pasture. The cows were in the front fields. Howard drove them along with him as he went. John met them at the top of the slope, with the field gate thrown wide open.

"Morning Dad, lovely day, may be hot later."

"Morning Son, just what I thought, d'you think we could get that last twelve acres baled today?"

"I think it'll need turning several times, if the sun settles in hot and we get a breeze later on."

"Let's get milked and have breakfast first then we'll see. Would Ling come and help? Bring the kiddies up to Mary for the day?"

"She's half expecting to come, the weather looked promising at six o'clock when I got out of bed."

"We'll give her a ring after breakfast, that van's useful isn't it? Pity she can't drive yet. Never mind I'll fetch her and the children after breakfast."

"She'll bring the strawberries most likely, she's got up early to get them picked, she's hoping to have a picnic in the hay."

"We'll have to ask Mary about that, she's the tea lady today, all the rest will be working."

After milking the cows were turned back on the front fields. John went to see them across the land and close the gate. Afterwards he leant on the gate for a few minutes, he loved this view, across the reservoir, the trees beyond and the roofs of Howards house and buildings. To the left the farm fields rising to the hill with the old mill and the pine trees on the skyline. Everything in that view promised him a fine day. A slight breeze had sprung up. The few clouds that were about were fluffy little white feathers in the sky. The sun, which had been hidden behind the trees, burned stronger every minute. A perfect day for the hay. John went back to the house for breakfast. Howard had nipped off in the farm car the moment milking was over. The car drove back up the yard as John reached the back door. Little Richard jumped out and came dashing towards him.

"Are we going to get the hay in today Grandad? Mummy thought we would when the sun came out, that's why we've come to help."

"Your Mum's quite right, we are going to get the hay, but first we're going to have breakfast. Here's Pete coming now so let's go along in." It was a family breakfast. Mary had a pan full of bacon and sausages on the Aga, and while Ling sat Richard and Sally Anne at the table, Howard and Peter washed at the sink and Angel made toast. Bill came across from the sheds to join them. While they ate they discussed the work. It was decided that Ling should take the small tractor and a turner and Howard should take a second set of tackle and follow her round half an hour later. That way the hay would be kept moving in the warm air. Hopefully by two o'clock the hay would be fit to bale.

After breakfast they all set to work. Mary on the dinner and keeping an eye on the children, Angel took on doing the hens. Peter and young Bill went across to wash down the milk parlour and leave all in readiness for afternoon milking. Howard and

Ling went with John to the workshop. They linked up the tractors, filled them with fuel and were soon ready for off. John worked with them and saw them away down the lane before eleven o'clock. The two tractors trundled along the lane through the gate and across a pasture field towards the hillside. When they reached the hayfield the sun was shining full on the mown grass. The field had only a very gentle slope but it was enough to catch the breeze. As they turned the thick hay the wind lifted the long grasses letting the air get through and the sun warm both the hay and the ground beneath. By dinnertime the field had been turned twice. After dinner it was nearly fit. They decided to turn it once more and then bale at about three o'clock when the sun was at its hottest.

All the family were in the field that sunny afternoon. Howard was soon working steadily round with the tractor and baler. On the bale sledge Peter was positioning the bales to come off the sledge in stacks of eight. John brought the big trailer down from the farm. He travelled slowly round the field with the Nuffield with trailer behind. Ling was on the trailer loading as she had always done before her marriage, John and young Bill began to load. It was slow work with only two of them but it meant that at least one good load would be safely picked up while the sun was still out, and the hay at it's very best. At half past four they were well on. More than half the field was baled and the courses of bales on the trailer were getting high.

Mary and Angel came across the field with young Richard racing ahead and Sally Anne in the pushchair. The two women carried baskets with a picnic tea for everyone. Work was abandoned and they all sat round on bales in the sunshine. The baskets contained packs of ham sandwiches, sausage rolls and a big pork pie cut into slices. One of Mary's fruit cakes was also sliced ready. There was a big bowl of strawberries, the sugar shaker and a pint of thick cream. A big spoon and a pile of little ones and a stack of fruit dishes were put out ready. Richard was wild with excitement.

"Are we all having tea in the field Nanny, all of us?"

"Yes Love we are because of this nice sunshine and we are all enjoying it."

"Are we going to pick up all the bales after tea Grandad? Can I help after tea?"

"I expect so but the bales are heavy so you will have to roll them along and let the grown-ups pick them up." Everyone sat round enjoying their tea. Ling and Howard and the children sat with bales against their backs eating and talking at the same time. Angel and Peter sat with Mary and John and young Bill. The talk was very much centred on the task in hand.

"How long will the baling take to finish Howard?" John was asking.

"Another hour and a half I should think. It's not as thick in the middle and the bouts will be shorter as we go on."

"Well I think if we finish loading this big load, take it up to the farm then Bill and I will milk so as not to get too far behind. When you finish bring the baler up to the house. Then we can all come down later with two tractors and the other two trailers and load all we can, take it up to the farm and call a halt until tomorrow. In the morning we can finish whatever's left. We've done really well today, there's no threat of rain, so no need to kill ourselves. Although it will be nice to see the end of haytime. D'you agree Peter?"

"Not half Uncle John. I've got other fish to fry during July." Everyone laughed at this and Angel went rosy red. She and Mary served out strawberries and cream for everyone and a little while after the party broke up. Howard was soon thudding out the bales again near the middle of the field. Mary and Angel collected the baskets, tea bottles and children and wended their way back up to the farm. Mary to her poultry and Angel to get the cows across the road ready for John and young Bill to come and milk them. John and Bill heaved Ling back on top of the load of bales and topped it up with another two courses of bales, roped it and set off for home. Ling rode up to the farm on top of the load which she had always loved to do.

Ling and Angel both helped with the milking and turning the

cows back into the field. Howard came in the yard gates with the baling tackle and Peter standing beside him on the tractor. Mary saw them coming and as usual the kettle was boiling and the teacups at the ready. Everyone trooped into the kitchen and found a chair to sink into. The hot tea quickly revived them all and within a quarter of an hour two tractors with trailers clanking behind them were going down the lane and across the fields. The sun was going down and the cooler air made working a lot easier. John took charge of one tractor, Howard the other. Ling climbed up to load Howard's trailer. Angel said she would do her best with the other, if Peter and John would show her how and load slowly. Young Bill helped Howard pitch bales to Ling. It took just over the hour to load the two loads. The men then roped them and Ling and Angel slid down the ropes to walk across the fields together and shut all the gates behind the two loads and follow them up the lane for home. They had left about one load in the field, but would easily unload all the hay at the barn, and pick up the last load from the field in one day tomorrow.

Everyone felt that the hay harvest was to all intents and purposes well and truly in and that some little celebration was needed. Peter and Howard went into Banworth in Howard's van and fetched them all a fish and chip supper, which was eaten round Mary's kitchen table. Little Richard was allowed to stay up but Mary had already tucked up Sally Anne in John's side of their double bed. They were all tired. After supper Peter took Angel for a walk under the new moon down to Bunny Warren. Howard and Ling loaded their little ones and set off for home. Bill rode out of the gates on his motorbike. Mary and John tidied the kitchen and walked round shutting up the poultry. Afterwards they went into the yard and smelt the wonderful smell of the loads of new mown hay, waiting to be unloaded into the dutch barn.

"It still gives me pleasure Love. To see the crops come in good, especially the hay. Good hay for the Jersey's feed in the long Winter. It's always a joy to feed round the cubicle houses in the Winter with green sweet-smelling hay. The cows have such an appetite for good hay. This year it's all come in good Lass. Not like some years when we mess about in the rain trying to get it as soon as we can. Anyway, bedtime now Girl, are you fit?"

"Yes John, I'm more than fit." She took his arm and they went back into the house.

"Leave the door for Loves Young Dream John."

"Surely, we'll lose them soon you know Lass, shall you mind?"

"We'll miss them, young folk in the house I mean."

"Never mind, back to Darby and Joan, not so bad after all, but will you mind?"

"Mind what?"

"Being just on our own again?"

"No Dear as long as I've got you, we'll get by and be happy won't we?"

"Oh yes we'll be happy."

Ling had loved being in the haytime, but she was glad to be finished with it. At home at Manor Farm the sun was ripening the strawberries. Howard painted two home-made 'Pick Your Own' signs and put them out for the weekend close to the Shop and Tearoom signs. Ling phoned the local paper and put an advert in the produce section. By the weekend all the last field of bales was carted and stacked under cover. John told Howard to have the weekend at home and help with the strawberry crop, the Hill Farm staff would cope with the milking.

Mary made a huge batch of scones in readiness. Howard and Ling again found that a surprising number of locals came to pick strawberries. They also found the local people picked the fruit carefully and left no litter. People who came from the town were more inclined to pull the plants about, mostly because of lack of understanding of plant care Howard felt. It was a busy and profitable weekend. They opened both days because of the fruit.

As Ling had hoped, people got hot and tired picking their strawberries and after paying for them, mostly folk put them in the car and went into the Tearoom for refreshment. Kitty put a sign outside the shop for 'Fresh Cream' 'With Your Strawberries', Mary who now had a licence to sell cream and farm butter, sent cartons of cream down to the Shop fridge. All of it was sold that weekend.

Howard and Ling enjoyed the strawberry harvest. It was like a rest cure after the hard toil of haymaking. They made friends with a lot of village folk over the next ten days. It was not a huge crop, but as is usual for the first year the fruit was all of good size, and with the lovely weather it was all in good condition. Ling picked twenty pounds for home and need and made them into jam. Mary and Angel also came and picked, paying the standard rate to keep the books straight. They picked over forty pounds between them, and jammed the whole lot on Hill Farm Aga. Mary put a few pots of jam in her own store cupboard, and Angel carted a few down to the cottage. The rest were stored in a cupboard in the dairy to sell in the Farm Shop later on.

"It's known as looking ahead," Mary assured Ling when she laughed about it. Mary was keeping an eye on her own patch of twenty blackcurrants in the garden. The bushes were loaded and when they were ripe Mary intended to jam the lot.

"I suppose you'll come raspberry picking when we've got them another year. And then sell the jam back through the shop as well?" Ling asked cheerfully.

"Oh yes and what about currant and gooseberries, are you going to do those later on? Not to mention Victoria plums, very popular and cheap to make Victoria plum jam." Mary looked full of energy as she spoke, and years younger with so much to interest her.

"Also of course we shall expect to be able to pinch your crab apples for crab apple jelly. The best ones are your side of the railway line."

"Never let's the grass grow under her feet our Ma, you know." Howard's voice came round the door as he overheard their conversation.

The raspberry patch was in fact looking good. The posts and wires were up ready and Howard had carted plenty of muck from the old heap behind the stackyard. With an occasional hoe through with the Mayfield tractor, the ground would be in prime fettle for the planting time in November. Ling's garden was also looking good. The old roses along the garden fence were in bloom and the scent was lovely. Summer lilies in their white perfumed elegance were in flower along the border beyond the lawn. In the narrow borders near the house pinks were coming out and adding to the scent. Over the porch door where every visitor to the tearoom passed in and out, a honey suckle scrambled. At the moment it was a mass of flowers. Almost everyone who came admired it and commented on the wonderful smell. Ling found time to weed through all her beds and to mow the lawns in between tearoom guests. She decided that another year she would grow some flowers for selling in the Shop. She and Kitty would discuss flowers so as not to clash in what they grew.

Ling wanted to grow wallflowers and sweet williams and also perhaps sweet peas. There was a space at the end of the garden where Howard had put cabbages for this time as a fill-in crop. Perhaps she could take over a strip of that area. The children loved to be in the garden with her, they had really taken to their new home. A little boy called David, whose family lived in a cottage on the Brushstoke green opposite, came with his Mother to pick strawberries. Richard and David became firm friends and were soon playing together in each others gardens. The only stipulation being that a grown-up must always be present when they crossed the main road.

When the strawberry crop was almost done Angel and Ling began to plan the wedding reception which was now only two weeks away. It was decided to have a buffet meal. A lunch with savouries on one big table, sweets on another and the wedding cake on a table in the big window, with a setting of flowers all round.

The gathering was to be only about thirty people in all, so there were plenty of chairs. It was decided to set up the little tea tables with a posy of flowers on each and a glass dish at the centre to hold four sets of cutlery wrapped in four pretty paper serviettes. People would be able to collect their choice of food and find a seat and a table without having to queue up for cutlery. The colour scheme was to be mainly shades of green, no pink because of clashing with the brides hair (Angel's suggestion). So it was that Ling bought white disposable cloths for the tables and pale green serviettes and they would use their own Beryl tearoom china. Kitty was doing all the flowers for the Tearoom from her own garden. She was going to do two large vases for the food table along the wall, posies to match for each small table and a big flower arrangement near the wedding cake, on a pedestal. It was a simple inexpensive scheme, but Mary knowing Kitty's ability with flowers, thought it would look lovely. Ling and Gorse were cooking the quiches and sausage rolls for the reception. Kitty was cooking a boiled ham and a large turkey, which would be cut up cold and served on large platters. Mary was making trifles and meringues and chocolate eclairs. The wedding cake was ordered from Angel's own home village paid for her by her parents. They were also providing the turkey and a whole ham for Kitty to cook. Kitty was also providing glass bowls of green salads from her garden, where everything was just at it's peak. Brushstoke W.I. was going to give the day and take charge of the Farm Shop. They would also explain to any would-be Tearoom customers why the Tearoom was closed for the day. Although Howard had put signs out to that effect for two weeks before the wedding.

In the middle of all these preparations Angel and Peter went on getting their future home ready. One morning at breakfast Peter asked John if he might have a morning off to take Angel to Birmingham to buy one or two very necessary items. John agreed at once but Mary seeing Angel blush rosy red, immediately jumped to the right conclusion.

"Not to be nosy Lass, but you're not going to buy a bed are

you?" Mary asked in her usual straight to the point fashion. At this Peter also went red in the face.

"Well yes we are, we didn't think we wanted a second-hand bed or mattress you see."

"You can't do that," said John startled out of sipping his cup of tea.

"Well you see we've got one for you, not second-hand." Mary reassured them, "There was this competition in the Farmer's Weekly and the prize was a bedroom suite. Well, you see, John won it; the bedroom suite that is. It was all because he described me as his greatest asset."

"Quite right Ma, you are all of us's greatest asset." Howard came in the door as he spoke, not having heard the previous part of the conversation.

"You mean you're going to give us a bedroom suite, surely that's not fair, if John won it you should have it?" Angel spoke for the first time.

"What's all this about a bedroom suite? Have I missed something?" Howard sat in a chair, spread his long legs out in front, and looked round enquiringly.

"Where is the bedroom suite now?" Asked Peter, somewhat lost in the present discussion.

"Oh you are a lot of softs," said Mary impatiently. "If you'd all hold your tongues and give me a chance to explain."

"Silence. All give way to my best asset, but in answer to you Peter, before Mary begins a long explanation, it's coming tomorrow." John was grinning from ear to ear.

"Oh be quiet, you too John, you're as bad as the youngsters! Now let me explain it to them from the beginning." Which she sat down and quietly did, making them understand that John had only entered the competition so that if he won, he and Mary would give them the bedroom suite as a wedding present for Bunny Warren. Angel's face lit up when she understood what Mary was saying to them.

"And you say it's coming tomorrow Aunt Mary. Will they bring it here?"

"Well they will come here first, I didn't think the big van would get down Bunny Warren lane. John suggested we let them unload it here in the big yard where there's plenty of room. If they put it on the trailer we could take it down to the cottage with the tractor. If you three men went down, you'd soon unload it. Angel could come and show you where she wants the things placed. Anyway they are coming in the morning."

Next morning at half past ten the furniture van arrived from Owen Owens. Welcome for it came in the form of everyone being there to see it arrive. John had put the tractor with a trailer on the back in the top yard. He explained the situation to the two young delivery men with the van. The driver turned his vehicle easily in the wide area of the top yard and they unloaded the bedroom suite on to the trailer. Angel was delighted with it and jumped up and down with excitement like a kid with a new toy. Especially she liked the pink rose buds and the brand new spring mattress.

"Aunt Mary what a lovely choice for the cottage, it's going to look perfect."

"That's just what we hoped Dear, it was hard to choose but that one seemed to fit the cottage."

"Let's all go down to Bunny Warren and see it in place." John drove the tractor down the lane and onto the main road, turning into the little green lane that led to Bunny Warren. Howard and Mary followed in the car, the rest rode on the trailer with the furniture. As they reached the little garden gate to Ling's old garden, it struck Mary that the little place looked lonely and forgotten. It would be good to have it occupied again. In the garden the wallflowers and daffodils were over, but Peter was keeping the grass mown and there were red roses climbing over the porch. The little borders were neatly weeded, Angel came often to do an hour in the garden.

In the cottage, Mary had not seen how hard Peter and Angel had been working to make it into a home again. Mary knew that they had not much money, but there were little homely touches everywhere. In the kitchen all the shelves were wiped spotless clean. The only furniture a small table and the two chairs from Hill Farm attic. But on the window-sill a vase of fresh roses and in the shelves a few plates, cups and saucers. On the table a small pile of tea-towels and table cloths neatly folded. In the sitting room, the settee from the attic at Hill Farm, a low chair and a small oak table on the carpet Kitty had given them. The things looked a little lost in the room compared with the standard of comfort Ling and Howard had had when they were here; all the same as she looked round, Mary could see all the little touches of home Angel had already added. The mirror over the mantle which Peter had hung after they bought it cheaply in the market. The bookcase from Angel's Mum, with Angel's books in it. Two or three pictures on the walls. Again a vase of flowers on the little table and another on the window-sill. An old rug before the fireplace. But everywhere was so clean, and in the grate a fire laid ready with a box of matches on the shelf above.

"Why my Dear, you've begun to make it look lovely, really homely, can I see upstairs?"

"Yes let's go up, they'll be bringing in the furniture now, let's go up first." Howard and Peter with a little help from John, manhandled the new suite upstairs. Fortunately the wardrobe top and bottom were lift-off parts, so it all came up the stairs fairly easily. It was an absolute pleasure to Mary to see Angel's joy in the lovely gift. As the men put up the bed and placed the dressing table and wardrobe in position, Angel left them for a minute and went into the bathroom. In the airing cupboard was her small stock of linen and blankets, and two new pillows that Peter had bought for her. A moment later she came back in the bedroom. The men had gone downstairs but Mary had waited. She helped Angel make up the bed and cover it with a lovely quality candlewick bedspread bought second-hand in Banworth market. Angel looked round with great pride, her eyes like stars.

"You and Uncle John will never know what this gift means to me, well to us I should say, but for the woman, a lovely home means so much. Doesn't it look really lovely Aunt Mary?"

There were tears in both women's eyes. Mary put her arms about Angel and kissed her gently. She suddenly felt so close to this girl who seemed to be able to be so happy with so little, in a time when most newly-weds were beginning to expect to have everything laid on as soon as they were married. Mary felt that Angel and Peter were a wonderful couple.

"It is lovely Dear, and you and Peter will make a very happy life here, I'm sure of it." The two women went downstairs and found the menfolk in the kitchen making a cup of coffee with dried milk. Again Mary noticed that in the cupboard Angel had stocked up with tea, coffee, sugar and a bottle of dried milk. A second-hand electric kettle stood on the work-top by the electric cooker, which had fortunately been left behind by Ling and Howard. What a blessing thought Mary, that Ling had wanted an Aga, of course they could afford it with Howard's money from his Uncle, and an Aga was a Godsend now the tearoom was up and running. What Angel needed now was a small fridge, she and John would have a think about that before the wedding. All these thoughts were inside Mary's head and she kept them to herself.

As Mary and John drove home Mary's mind was very much on the two young ones. John noticing how quiet she was, glanced down at her serious expression.

"What are you plotting Lass, you've gone very quiet and serious, had something upset you?"

"No John, not really, just that Angel is such a lovely girl, she's making a real little home on very little money at the cottage, she told me that you and I would never know how much that bedroom suite means to her. And all over the house, just little homely things that only cost a pound or two. You know I've got a set of three saucepans for an electric cooker. I never use them now we have the Aga. I shall look them out and give them a good clean up and put them ready for Angel to take down to the cottage."

"That would be nice, Angel's a good girl, she always appreciates anything we do for her. But they will enjoy struggling to build a home together. We did, if you can remember that far back."

"It wasn't that far back John, and yes I do remember, and most of all putting all those shillings in that old ginger jar to save up and buy a hoover. It took over two years and I had to brush the carpets by hand until we got it. Not that we had many carpets in those days." Mary chuckled cheerfully and got out of the car and went indoors to put the dinner on to cook. John coming in behind her said firmly,

"In any case what Angel really needs next is a small fridge, I shall get them one at the electric shop in Banworth, they often have them there not too dear."

"Now you're talking, how clever of you to notice and pick that out as being necessary. I had thought just the same, but most men wouldn't have noticed."

"Ah well you see, I'm not just a pretty face." John grinned like the cat that's had the cream.

STRAWBERRIES AND CREAM

Chapter 13

Richard the Lionheart

STRAWBERRIES AND CREAM

Chapter 13

Richard the Lionheart

Just over a week before the wedding, Howard and Ling had the Friday at home. It was a wet day. The rain had been falling steadily when Howard had gone across to Hill Farm early to milk the cows. After breakfast John had called off all outdoor work for the day. Back home at Manor Farm, Howard and Ling had decided to make all the preparations they could for the wedding. As it was Friday both Shop and Tearoom were closed. In the morning Ling made her shopping list ready for the following week and prepared as much of the decoration and layout for the reception as possible. Paper napkins were folded, cruets were polished, glasses which had been hired from Banworth were counted and polished. Vases were put out ready for Kitty to fill with flowers. Oasis was cut to fit the little green table decoration bowls lent by Angel's Mother. By the time Ling had done all she felt she could so far ahead, it was time for a sandwich lunch. Ling set sandwiches on a tray. Howard picked Sally Anne out of her playpen and sat her in her little chair. Richard came down from the toys in his own bedroom.

"I want to be outside after Dad, I want to plough the bottom of the rickyard, where I started yesterday. It's nearly stopped raining, if I put my wellies on can I be outside Mummy?" Richard had a little toy tractor and a plough which John had made for him in Hill Farm workshop.

"Yes you can, but wash your hands first, Mummies got a tray of goodies for us to eat in the sitting room."

They spent a happy hour with the children. Sally Anne was beginning to learn how to feed herself. She could hold a little sandwich now and much of it would find it's way to her mouth.

While they ate they discussed what else they could do to further the wedding preparations during the afternoon.

"Well we could put all the drinks on the shelves just down the cellar steps, it's far the best place to have them handy."

"Good idea, that number of bottles would clutter up the room or the washing-up area, especially with the tearoom being open this weekend."

"We'd need to brush down the cellar shelves and steps but that needs doing anyway. Let's have a go at that while there's two of us to tackle it."

"Can I still play outside, if I'm very carefully Mummy?" Richard's eyes were wide and eager.

"Yes I think he could, don't you Howard? If he comes in sometimes to let us know he's OK. But just in the rickyard only Richard. The yard gate to the road is locked as the tearoom's closed. You don't go near the main road OK?"

"Can I go now then Mummy?" Richard was wriggling in his eagerness.

"No wait a minute poppet, Sally Anne's been awake all morning, she can go in the pram and I'll put it under the dutch barn, close by you Richard, in the dry. So you will keep an eye on her, she'll most likely go to sleep. You must stay near her and come and say if she cries. will that be OK?"

"Oh yes I'll be really carefully of her." Richard was learning to enjoy small responsibilities.

————————

Twenty minutes later with the tray washed up and brooms, dustpan and cloths at the ready, Howard and Ling made a start on the cellar. The cellar door was under the stairs, it had a big key which hung on a nail by the kitchen door. Fortunately there was an electric light on the stairs and another in the big underground room below. Ling tied a scarf round her hair to keep the dust off. Soon they were busily brushing down shelves, stairs and beamed ceiling. It was quite a dusty, dirty job which made them cough in the dusty atmosphere. Ling was never sure how long they had been working, but she began to feel dry-mouthed and thirsty.

"Let's go up and get a glass of orange and have a break from this dust, it's dried up my throat."

"OK let me just get this last bunch of cobwebs, then the ceiling's done. While you get a drink ready I'll nip and have a look at the kids." Ling started up the steps. Suddenly the stairs light went out.

"Oh damn, I think the bulb's gone Howard, take care how you come."

"It's alright the main one down here is still on. Carry on I'm right behind you."

As Ling reached the top two steps everything happened very quickly. A hand came through the cellar door in front of her. the hand was big, the fingers spread wide, and she felt a sudden hard push in the chest. She immediately fell backwards into Howard coming up behind her. The door in front of her slammed shut and she heard the key turn in the lock as she fell. Howard caught the full force of Ling falling, luckily he was holding the rail and managed to cling on and grab Ling with his free hand. They both fell on the steps, but did not go to the bottom. Anger was Howard's first emotion.

"Sit here Love, did you see anyone?"

"Only a big hand came through the door and pushed me back."

"My god, are you all right? Some young fool from the village larking about. I'll give 'em what for." He climbed up the steps and banged on the door with both fists.

"Open this door. Stop buggering about you idiots. Open this door." There was no reply. Howard tried again and again but no one came. Howard's anger steadied, Ling was looking so frightened.

"Don't panic Darling, let's be quiet and listen, see what we can hear." He put his ear to the door and listened. He thought he could hear the sound of men's voices and the sound of something being dragged along. Suddenly louder, one voice sounded rough and angry.

"They've shut us down here deliberately, there's two, I can hear their voices. I'm afraid we're stuck for the moment Darling. The exit to the garden has a stone slab right across the top. I'll never lift it from underneath."

"But Howard," Ling's voice was shaking but she was determined not to break down. "What do you think they want? What about the children? Oh Howard pray God Sally Anne went to sleep and Richard doesn't come in." She was white with fear for the children.

"I think we must be being burgled Darling, I can't think of anything else."

"But we haven't got anything small of value, no precious silver or china. Only the TV and your office stuff."

"Now Sweetheart, we must try and be calm, they may open the door before they go. The police always say they want to get away as quick as possible. Shall I bang again or shall we wait and listen for the key in the lock?"

"Bang again Howard. It may make them go away quickly, but it's the children Howard. What about the children?"

In the stackyard Richard went to peep in Sally Anne's pram, she was fast asleep.

"I'd better just telled Mummy," he reluctantly left his tractor and went into the main yard. The first thing he saw was a black car parked up close outside the main gate. He went on into the little yard by the back porch. The door stood wide. Suddenly he heard a strange rough angry voice.

"Get a bloody shift on you slow young bugger, time we was bloody out of this dump." Then Richard heard a loud repeated banging and then his Daddy's voice also shouting and full of anger.

"Open this damn door. Unlock this door at once, you're frightening my wife." Richard stopped dead in his tracks. Someone had shut his Daddy and Mummy down the cellar. The man with the angry voice must have done it. He slipped back outside the door. All was quiet now. Richard felt very frightened, but Mummy said that boys must be brave and look after little girls. Little girls, Sally Anne. He must get back to Sally Anne and find someone to help. Nanny and Grandad, if only Nanny was here, or Uncle Peter. They wouldn't let that man hurt Mummy and Daddy. He crept back down the steps and along the yard, his rubber soled wellies making no sound. It was spitting with rain still but not much. Richard turned the corner out of sight in the stackyard. He ran to the pram. She was still fast asleep. He must get Nanny, he couldn't go across the main road. He'd have to go across the fields, but he mustn't leave Sally Anne. Could he put her safe? If that nasty man found her and tooked her away! Tears threatened him at the thought. He gave a big gulp. What about Daddy's workshop? He knew the key was under the tile. If he pushed the pram in Daddy's workshop he could lock the door and hide the key back under the stone tile. Then the man with the angry voice couldn't take her away. The workshop door opened into the stackyard, the man wouldn't see him. Small fingers found the key. The little grubby hand shook as he put the key in the lock. The door opened easily. He went for the pram. He struggled with the brake but managed to release it. He wheeled the pram slowly, like Mummy always did when Sally Anne was fast asleep. Carefully up the step and inside. Brake on again, Mummy always did that. He peeped in the pram. A sigh of relief, she was still asleep. He crept out and locked the door, hid the key under the slate and ran.

He ran across the stackyard and wriggled under the fence, stinging his knees on the nettles. Tears stung in his eyes as he ran along the hedge-line of the Mound field. On the other side he couldn't open the gate. There was a hole in the hedge, he knelt down and began to scramble through. A sharp thorn dug in his knee. He cried out and tears ran down his cheeks. Oh how he wanted his Mummy, but Mummy was shut in the cellar and he was the only one who could fetch Nanny. It was much further when you were by yourself. At last he saw the railway line ahead. Only one gate, and then the tunnel. THE TUNNEL, he was very frightened of the tunnel. It was dark in the middle. When Mummy was here it was fun in the tunnel. They would shout out and Mr. Echo would shout back. When Mummy was here. But Mummy was shut down in the cellar and that nasty man was in the house. And he must get to Nanny. He scrambled through another hedge, tearing his shorts on the thorns. A bramble scratched his face and legs. He rubbed his eyes with grubby hands because he could hardly see the tunnel for tears. There was water in the tunnel, the rain had been long and heavy. Richard's little hands clenched. He didn't think he could go in. He took a deep breath, Nanny was at the other end of the tunnel. Boys must be brave. Sally Anne was locked in the workshop. Daddy and Mummy were locked in the cellar. Little hands tight clenched, arms tight to his sides, lips pressed shut, eyes wide, he took the first few steps. Perhaps if he kept saying Nanny and Grandad in his head, like speaking to Jesus when he said his prayers. He heard the words over and over in his head, but not a sound came from his tight little mouth. He kept putting one welly in front of the other. Then the water came over the top of his boots, wet and squelchy in his socks. What if he drownded? But he could see the end of the tunnel, the dark was almost behind him. The little patch of light grew bigger, and then he saw it .... one of Grandad's cows eating grass. A great sob nearly choked him, but he was out. The stile by the closed gate was there in front of him. He squeezed through the bottom rail. He was in the field, the field where Uncle Peter had come down with him on the sledge, when the snow was there.

His wellies were full of water, he left one behind in the mud by the stile. His courage failed him and sobs again burst out of his nose and eyes. He pulled his welly out of the mud and hopped back to the stile. Sitting on the bottom step he emptied both boots and dragged them back on. There were cows everywhere munching grass contentedly, they took no notice of him, to him they were old friends. He scrambled to his feet, dashing the tears away with dirty hands. He tried to run up the steep slope but his little legs were too heavy, they would only move very slowly. Gradually it became less steep, he tried to run again but couldn't get his breath, sobs again rose in his throat, his nose and eyes were running all the time now. Where was his hanky? He found it and could hear his Nanny's voice saying 'Have a good blow Darling, you'll find it will cheer you up.' He stopped in his tracks and had a good blow, it calmed him. Soon he was at the top stile. He was too tired to climb over and struggled through the lowest bar. The lane, again, Nanny's voice came to him clear in his head 'Look both ways Richard, mind the cars.' He looked and looked again, no cars, he crossed, starting to run again, his legs felt better now, it was easier on the hard surface of the farm drive. He was up the drive and by the back door. He reached as high as he could but couldn't reach the latch. His tired legs gave way and he sank down on the mat, lifting both hands to bang again and again on the door.

John and Mary were in the sitting room.

"Was that the back door?" John raised his eyes from the account book he was working on sitting at the table.

"I'll look and I'll put the kettle on. Young Bill and Peter could do with a cup of tea I dare say."

When Mary opened the door, for a second she thought no one was there. Then she looked down.

"John, John, come quickly it's little Richard." Richard felt himself lifted into those dear arms. His arms came up and wound tightly round Nanny's neck.

"Oh Nanny I never thought I'd founded you." Mary soothed the little shaking body, holding him firmly against her old work dress.

"There little Love, you have founded me. It'll be all lovely now, alright now Poppet. But where's Mummy and Daddy?" Mary carried him through and sat down in John's big chair, her arms still tight about him.

"Well a nasty man comed, he locked Mummy and Daddy in the cellar. So I locked Sally Anne in Daddy's workshop and hided the key, cos Mummy said not to leave her, and I thoughted she'd be safe, in case the nasty man tooked her away. I couldn't bring her pram across the fields and in the tunnel. I did hided the key under the stone where Daddy does, then I comed to find you, but my legs got tired. I did try to be brave but there was water in the tunnel and it filled my wellies and it was dark. So dark, Mummy wasn't there so we couldn't shout to Mr. Echo, and .... Oh Nanny it was so dark. It made me cry, but in the end I had a good blow, like you said and then I cheerded up."

John was already at the back door meeting young Bill coming across the yard with Peter coming just behind him.

"Young Richard's here and he's come on his own from Manor Farm. Sounds like a break-in. Can you go over in the car quick if I phone the police?" Peter took in the situation at a glance.

"Richard says they locked Ling and Howard in the cellar. So he put Sally Anne's pram in Howard's workshop and locked the door. Hid the key under Howard's usual stone."

"Did the nasty man see you Darling?"

"No I crepted away when I heard the nasty man shouting, and Daddy shouting through the cellar door."

"We'll get over there, you phone the police Uncle John, but I expect they're long gone." A moment later Bill and Peter were driving out of the yard gates and heading towards Banworth, turning left over the railway bridge towards Brushstoke. John and Mary concentrated their attention on Richard.

"You have been a brave little boy, Nanny and Grandad are so proud of you." Mary patted Richard's back while John pulled off his wellies and wet socks.

"Now Grandad's going to run you a warm bath with some of Nanny's lovely green bubbles in the water. Nanny will find you some clean clothes. Peter and Bill will let Mummy and Daddy out of the cellar and fetch Sally Anne back in the house. And a big policeman will come and take the nasty man away."

Soon they were in the bathroom. Mary peeled off the torn muddy clothes and lifted him in the warm water. He gasped at the pain of his scratches in the water. Mary saw him bite his lips, determined not to cry. She felt tears in her own eyes as she watched his brave, weary little face. Carefully she sponged him down and removed all the dirt and mud from his feet. Then she picked him out in a big warm towel, pulled the plug on the bath and carried him downstairs. John had found an old shirt, well shrunk, in the airing cupboard, and a pair of old school shorts of Howard's long back. Mary took her tweezers and lifted the thorn out of Richard's knee. She dried him and dressed him in the odd garments. He stayed on her knee, held closely in the safety of her big comfortable lap. John brought a tray of tea, pink and white sponge cake and hot milk for Richard. He ate and drank and then almost immediately fell asleep in her arms. John looked at the little white sleeping face.

"What a proper little Radford he is. Fancy him managing all that way on his own. God bless him. I'll ring Manor Farm number now and make sure all's well there Lass."

When Peter and Bill arrived at Manor Farm, a police car was parked outside the yard gate. The two policemen had just got there and were about to climb the yard gate which they had found to be locked. Peter and Bill climbed out of the car, having parked a few yards further up the road on the grass verge, the Sergeant waited for them,

"You Mr. Radford of Hill Farms nephew Sir?"

"That's right and this is Bill, one of our farm staff. We thought it safer if we both came."

"Quite right Sir, we'll all go in together, is the Lad alright, the little boy who went for his Granny?"

"Yes, yes, he's fine I think, very frightened of course."

When they were all inside the yard Peter looked round and

seeing no one turned to Bill.

"You know the workshop Bill? Well Sally Anne's in there in her pram, could you go and get her? You know where Howard keeps the key?"

"Oh yes I'll get her." Bill hurried off down towards the rickyard.

"Now Sir, we'll go first, you come and show us the cellar door." The two policemen moved across the yard and up to the back door. It stood wide open and in the kitchen/tearoom all looked exactly as usual. They moved on into the passageway. The door immediately opposite was the cellar door. At once there came a banging on the other side of it.

"Here Sir, wait a minute, hold on."

"We're here Howard, cavalry's arrived." Peter added his voice to reassure Howard and Ling. The key was turned in the door and a moment later their ordeal was over. Ling's first words told everything.

"Oh Peter, thank God you've come! Richard! Can you see if Richard and Sally Anne are alright? He was playing in the stackyard but it was ages ago."

"Richard's fine, he's with Aunt Mary, he went for help across the fields. Young Bill's gone to fetch Sally Anne in. Richard locked her in the workshop for safety and hid the key back under the slate." Ling who had kept up well for the last hour, promptly burst into tears.

"Now, you find the kettle constable, these folks need some hot tea. Come through and sit down a minute Mrs. Radford, and then perhaps if you should feel up to it Mr. Radford, you could walk through and tell me if there's anything missing. There's no one about now, scarpered off quick I reckon."

Howard was feeling calmer now in the knowledge that the children were unhurt. At that moment Bill came in the back door pushing Sally Anne's pram. She was lying back obviously just waking up. Ling picked her up and held her close, relief in her every movement.

"Hello Baby that's a good girl, Oh Howard I think she's slept all through it."

The police were there for some time. The thieves had taken some of Howard's new office equipment and a small amount of silver and china from the bedroom, including two bracelets and a necklace which had belonged to Ling's Mother. In the kitchen, the new electric toaster and the most distressing thing of all the still boxed and wrapped china tea service which they had bought as a wedding present for Angel and Peter, the police found two sets of very clear prints. For Ling and Howard, but especially for Ling, it was the dirty feeling of violation of her home which hurt most. They had never locked the door at Bunny Warren or at Manor Farm, except when they were actually going out somewhere. It was a very upsetting thing to happen, Ling felt unable to let Sally Anne out of her sight. So when at last Peter and Bill went off to milk and the police had gone and Howard suggested that they drive over to Hill Farm to fetch the hero of the hour, little Richard, Ling still kept the little girl close in her arms.

At Hill Farm when they went into the kitchen, Mary came to greet them. Seeing Ling's white face above the now sleeping child in her arms, Mary took the little girl and gave her into John's care. Then Mary put her arms round Ling, held her close, gently patting her back. Ling burst into fresh floods of tears.

"Oh Mum, Oh Mum it's all so dreadful, they were in our house going through our things. They could have hurt the children, so easily, they could have hurt the children."

"But they didn't Love. And your little Richard was so brave, coming all this way to get help. And putting Sally Anne safe. He isn't quite five yet you know. We, John and I, were so proud of him. It's tired him out, he's fast asleep in our bed. Come and sit down Dear, tell us all about it, did you hear their voices or see anything?"

"No very little, it was a big rough hand which pushed me in the chest, then the door banged and we got locked in."

"I wonder if Richard saw anything?" John queried in a quiet voice.

"That's what the policeman wondered, he's going to come and see him tomorrow, when Richard's had time to get over it a bit. We thought we could get him to tell us all about it and perhaps pick up something from there. But to tell the truth I'm so tired Mum I feel as though someone had hit me with a cricket bat, over and over as hard as they could." At that moment Peter came in with hot drinks on a tray. Ling was soon sipping hers and some colour came back into her face. Mary watched thankfully thinking that talking about it was helping Ling get over the shock. Later Angel came, she had been over with Kitty for the day, and of course she had to be told all over again what had happened.

Later they went upstairs to fetch Richard. He opened his eyes sleepily.

"Hello Mummy is it hometime?"

"Yes Darling it's hometime. We've come to fetch our brave big boy home. Have you had a nice sleep?"

"Yes and I've been in Nanny's bed. Did the policeman catch that nasty man?"

"Not yet, but the nasty man has gone away and he won't be back."

"Well I sawed his car, by our gate it was, it was black. Has it gone Mummy? Did the policeman find it?"

"No Darling, what was it like, did you notice?" A small frown came between Richard's eyebrows, and he pursed up his mouth.

"Well it was black, not very big and I saw my letters on it."

"Your letters Darling?"

"Yes, you know. The letters in my brick box. The two you tolded me were mine. RR."

"You mean that the car had your letters in the number plate?" Howard spoke for the first time.

"Yes Daddy, but not side by side."

"Ah you mean with numbers and other letters in between."

"Yes I think so Daddy."

"Forget it now Son, hometime." They went downstairs, Howard carrying Richard, Ling took Sally Anne from John and both children sat in the back with Ling for the journey home. At home the children settled in bed easily and seemed quite unperturbed. This did a lot to reassure Ling. She and Howard left extra lights on and were soon in bed as well.

"Alright now Sweetheart?" Howard was anxious about her.

"Yes, yes, I'm fine. We've just got to forget it, put it all behind us, haven't we? Otherwise the wedding will be spoiled."

"That's my girl, let's cuddle down now and get to sleep."

"Yes let's, only one thing Howard, new locks. Could we put new locks on the back and front doors do you think?"

"I'd already decided that, I'll see to it first thing in the morning. Alright Precious?"

"Yes alright Howard." But it was a long time before they dropped off to sleep.

———————

STRAWBERRIES AND CREAM

Chapter 14

All's Well That Ends Well

STRAWBERRIES AND CREAM

Chapter 14

All's Well That Ends Well

The rest of the week was very showery but the heavy rain was over. It was almost too hot when the sun was out, but to Ling it was a joy. She was busy tidying the garden and the house for the wedding. The police had not caught the burglars in spite of the black car with the two R's in the number plate. The sergeant had told Howard and Ling that he thought that they had most likely been opportunists who had stopped at the farm in the first place hoping to get tea, seen the door open and come in to pinch what they could pick up quickly. They must have heard a noise in the cellar, heard Ling and Howard on the stairs. That would have put the wind up them, and what followed was on the spur of the moment, because they were frightened.

Ling and Howard found themselves determined to put it all behind them. The sunshine helped a good deal. All the family were preparing for the wedding. On the Wednesday Angel went home to her family to get ready at that end. John took Mary into Banworth where she bought a fresh spray of pink artificial roses for her large brown hat. She had already bought a full skirted brown dress with a tiny pattern of cream roses together with a new handbag, shoes and gloves. The hat was an old favourite in which she felt comfortable. Mary usually wore navy or plain brown, but John, for whom she dressed up in the outfit to get his opinion, thought she looked a picture. John himself, and Howard who was best man, were going to stick to their best suits which had been sent to the dry-cleaners. New ties, well polished shoes and buttonholes completed their outfits. Especially as in this case John did not have to give the bride away. Ling's outfit was a soft green dress and a small hat made of dyed green feathers.

Howard called her his little greenfinch when he saw her in it, but it did look sweet perched on top of her head, with her dark curls curling up round it. Richard who was to be a page, had a new dark suit and his first grown-up haircut. He looked like a small grown-up man as he stood tall and straight for Ling's inspection. The only wedding touch, the neat little bow tie and the narrow frill down the front of his white shirt.

Kitty brought the wedding cake over on Thursday in the back of her car. The tearoom was already set for the great day. Howard carried the cake in, it was a large square single layer, beautifully decorated with lemon yellow roses and gold ribbon bows, nesting in sprays of green rose leaves. They placed it in position on the table in the big tearoom window. The table was covered down to the floor with a white lace cloth made years before by Kitty's Grandmother.

Kitty came again on the Friday, her car was loaded with flowers. When they were all carried into the kitchen the scent was glorious. Kitty and Ling spent the afternoon decorating the whole room. The result was like a Summer cottage garden, with flowers everywhere in welcome to tomorrow's guests. Also on the Friday Howard and Ling had visits from members of the family who were sharing the task of making the food for the reception. Some of the tasks would have to be tackled on Saturday morning early. Such as putting cream into eclairs and meringues and on top of the trifles. Howard would bring the cream from the farm after early morning milking. Howard and Ling knew they would have time to whip the cream and use it to decorate the food because the wedding was not until twelve o'clock. Over in Angel's village, she and her Mother decorated the Church helped by half the village folk, where Angel's family had lived all their lives.

Most of the Radfords spent Friday morning getting ready for the wedding in one way or another, but in the evening Mary and John held a little buffet party for all the family. Ling and Howard, with everything done ready for Saturday, went up to the farm in the van taking the children with them. Kitty and Jim came leaving Simon and Nicky with a child-sitter. Charles and Gorse didn't come, they felt it was too difficult and they were, in any case, expecting Barbara, Gorse's sister, who was coming off the evening train to stand in for Gorse and Charles all day Saturday in caring for the children and the farm animals. Kitty and Jim brought Angel over with them. Everyone at Hill Farm had, as usual, been working very hard. Peter much preferred a family evening with Angel and all the others to any sort of stag party. In any case he never had been much of a drinker.

It proved to be a real Radford event. A snacks meal on Mary's kitchen table followed by card and paper and pencil games in the sitting room or time spent in the garden, because it proved to be a warm and pleasant evening. The men talked of farming and the progress of the crops, the Farm Shop and the Tearoom. In spite of the burglary everyone felt that all the family were beginning to see small increases in their farm incomes. The women talked about the wedding, their clothes, the flowers and the food. After a while talk turned to strawberries and fruit generally. They all felt that they had done well with the choice of strawberries, and that raspberries would do equally well and that they ought also to take on board black and red currants and goosberries. Especially as the garden tractor was proving so helpful with weed control. All told it was a very happy family evening, and Mary and John were aware for the first time of how much the family had been drawn together by the purchase of Manor Farm and the new ventures in which they all had a share of the work and the profits.

Toward the end of the evening John opened some wine and Mary carried in the tray of glasses. John stood up, glass in hand.

"I know we are not a drinking family, but this evening I want to make two toasts. The first is to Peter and his lovely Angel and to the their happiness together within our family. Will you raise your glasses to Peter and Angel?" Everyone echoed his words.

"The second is to Howard and Ling and their courage in buying Manor Farm and opening our two new projects there. All of us are already beginning to benefit from the Farm Shop and the Tearoom, one way or another. Both Mary and I have no doubt that later on all the children will benefit in turn from both these ventures. So everyone, the second toast is Howard and Ling and all our farm enterprises." Again all the glasses were lifted. Ling felt a great warmth towards John and all the family.

Soon the party broke up. Peter and Angel slipped away into the dusk of the garden for a very special goodnight kiss.

"I love you so much Precious, I promise to do everything I can to make you happy." Peter's arms were close about her, her lovely hair falling against his shoulder.

"I know you will Darling, I'll never sleep tonight, I'm so excited and Mary's party's only made me worse. Oh Peter we are so lucky. The family, the cottage, the farm, everything. I'm so happy, you know that don't you?"

"Yes Sweetheart I know that," he bent to kiss her again.

"See you tomorrow in Church," she whispered.

"See you tomorrow, I'll be waiting." He took her hand and led her back into the house.

———————————

The Church was full, the sunlight streamed in through the windows. The organ burst forth with Here Comes The Bride. All the family turned to see Angel come up the aisle on her Father's arm. Her dress was a lovely full skirted crinoline looped up with little bunches of yellow rose buds. Her veil fell from a tiny cap trimmed with seed pearls and rose buds. In her hands she carried a bouquet of yellow roses, lily of the valley and trailing fern. Peter drew in his breath as she came up to his side. Their eyes met and his cup of joy was filled. The little hand on to which he slipped the wedding ring was brown and firm from her work on the farm and in the garden at Bunny Warren. His own was equally hard and work-worn, but he felt nothing but pride in their hard work and future together. The service passed in a sort of dreamy happy daze for them both. As they walked down the aisle as man and wife they both looked so happy, that Mary for one felt her eyes fill with joy. Ling and Howard, Kitty and Jim, left their children to travel home with Mary and John, slipping away quickly to be at the tearoom and have everything ready. Daisy and two friends of hers were there already and had preparations well in hand. Soon cars were pulling up in the big farmyard and the guests came flooding in. Bride and Groom were first and stood by the door to welcome everyone. All the guests enjoyed the home-made food. Everyone knew everyone else so conversation was easy and full of laughter. Toasts were drunk, speeches very short (John told them that farmers never say much!) were made. Before the end Peter and Angel slipped up to change, and came down again to make their rather shy farewells.

The honeymoon destination, just a few days, was a well kept secret. Their car had been carefully hidden in the Plough car park over the road. At the last moment they ran away across the road, into the car park and into their car and away, with no tin cans tied anywhere. Peter drove off up through Brushstoke, past the Church and School and on down the hill. He was laughing all over his face.

"We made it Darling, d'you think anyone knows?"

"Aunt Mary and Uncle John, no one else."

"Well they are as safe as houses."

"That's what I thought." Angel was laughing too. Ten minutes later Peter drew off the main road and a moment after they pulled up outside Bunny Warren. The little house and garden were full of welcome. Howard put the car further down the lane out of sight. They carried their cases to the door. Peter opened it with the old key from under a stone. He turned to lift his bride over the old flagstone doorway.

"Welcome home Mrs. Radford."

"Oh Peter, what fun, what better place for our honeymoon than our own little house." She clung to him, her arms about his neck. He set her down and went back for the suitcases. In the kitchen on the table was a card, a basket of eggs and a big can of

215

milk. The card read as follows .... With love to an Angel from the 'In-laws.' Everything else is in cupboard or fridge. Fridge is wedding gift .... !!

Angel and Peter laughed aloud, both were looking round the kitchen. Both saw the dark green draped rug. Peter pulled it away, underneath was a white fridge.

"What a lovely surprise, let's look inside." Angel opened the fridge door, it was full, a cold cooked chicken, a pie which looked like apple, a trifle, bacon, butter lard and green salad. At the top was one of Mary's cartons of cream and two loaves of bread. Peter opened the store cupboard, tins of food, jam, honey, tea, coffee, sugar and every sort of food filled the shelves. Two tins held biscuits and a cake.

"How lovely, they are so good to us."

"Let's put the kettle on and make a cuppa, I hardly ate a bite at that reception," Peter took the electric kettle and filled it.

"Home," he said, "our very own home at last." They enjoyed the tea and the quiet of the cottage after the noise and bustle of the day. Afterwards they unpacked upstairs and then came down and went into the garden. The orchard was full of birdsong and the little stream gurgled along through the buttercups and cow parsley.

"I'll make a seat for down here, Howard and Ling had one. It's a nice place to sit." For now they sat on the grass listening to the sounds of evening all round them.

"I've a little gift for you my Love, it's down there in the grass by the bank." Angel leant down by the stream and Peter thought how glorious her hair was against the green of her dress.

"Where is it? I can't see anything."

"Just a bit to the right."

"Oh Peter, Peter it's a rabbit, a little fat stone rabbit, like the one that always used to live here. Oh what a wonderful present, what shall we call him?"

"Just Bun I should think, so that we keep up the tradition. Shall we hide the key under him?"

"Of course, that's what it has always been. Key under Bun at

Bunny Warren."

"Come and pull me up, we'll put JUST BUN by the door make a bit of supper and sample that new bedroom suite."

"Oh Peter I'm so very happy." They linked arms and went back into the cottage, sitting the little rabbit in his usual place as they went by. The door closed and they began their new life together.

THE END